The New Book of Forms

A Handbook of Poetics

Lewis Turco

The New Book of Forms

A Handbook of Poetics

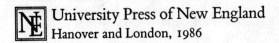 University Press of New England
Hanover and London, 1986

University Press of New England
Brandeis University
Brown University
Clark University
University of Connecticut
Dartmouth College
University of New Hampshire
University of Rhode Island
Tufts University
University of Vermont

© 1986 by University Press of New England

Printed in the United States of America

LIBRARY OF CONGRESS CATALOGING IN PUBLICATION DATA
Turco, Lewis.
   The new book of forms.
   Expanded revision of: Book forms published in 1968.
   1. Poetics.   2. Versification.   I. Turco, Lewis.
Book forms.   II. Title.
PN1042.T78   1986   808.1   86-40116
ISBN 0-87451-380-4
ISBN 0-87451-381-2 (pbk.)

John Crowe Ransom, "Bells for John Whiteside's Daughter," from *Selected Poems, Third Edition, Revised and Enlarged,* copyright Alfred A. Knopf, Inc., reprinted by permission of Alfred A. Knopf, Inc.

For old friends:
Charlie Davis and Hyatt Waggoner,
and in memory of Loring Williams.

Contents

Preface

Like the original *Book of Forms,* which was published in 1968 and subsequently became the standard in its field, *The New Book of Forms: A Handbook of Poetics* is intended as a text and reference work for students and teachers of poetry in general and of verse composition in particular. Although the accent is on the forms of poetry, this volume contains all the information essential to a study of poetics ranging from the Middle Ages to the present.

The volume begins with a "Handbook of Poetics" arranged in "levels"—the typographical, the sonic, the sensory, and the ideational levels. These chapters survey the two *modes* of writing—prose and verse—and various prosodic and metrical systems, clarify terms such as *rhythm, cadence,* and *meter,* and provide clear explanations of the processes and methods of versification. Figurative language is defined and discussed, as are considerations such as diction, style, syntax, and overtone.

The second part of the volume is called "The New Book of Forms," and it begins with a "Form-Finder Index" in which all the forms contained in the volume are listed and divided, first into *specific forms,* and then into *general forms.* Under "specific forms" there are further subdivisions, beginning with *one-line forms* and working through to *two hundred ten-line forms.*

Should you wish to know the form of a poem you are studying, rather than leaf through all the forms in the book, you can first determine (1) the *rhyme scheme* of the poem or stanza in question and (2) its *meter.* Then you can (3) *count the lines in the form* and turn to the Form-Finder. There, under the appropriate heading, will be a short list of stanza and whole poem patterns, from which you can determine the exact name of the poem form in question.

Similarly, should a student of verse composition wish to use a form of a specific length, he or she can consult the Form-Finder to discover an interesting structure. Many students find there is no quicker way to improve their writing than through formal experimentation and attempts to solve specific technical problems.

Following the Form-Finder is the most comprehensive compilation of the verse forms traditionally used in Anglo-American prosody ever gathered between covers. Over three hundred forms are listed alphabetically, dozens of which have been added for this edition of *The New Book of Forms*.

Our heritage of forms is rich. We are heirs not only of British metrical systems, but also of systems derived from Europe, the Middle East, and Asia. Our history of verse forms goes back to the Normans, the Anglo-Saxons, and the Celts, and we have derived much from the systems of the Hebrews, the Greeks, the Italians, and the French. The verse forms set forth here have all been utilized by poets of the English-speaking world. During every period of English letters, craftsfolk and bards have explored the possibilities of the formal structure of verse and extended the range of those structures.

This new version of *The New Book of Forms* adds a feature the original edition did not have: *examples of poems written in each form by poets from all periods*. Each form is described succinctly in prose. Where necessary, a unique schematic diagramming system lays the pattern of the form out on the page so that its structure is clear. Generally, there follows at least one poem exemplifying the form, always in a modern English version; or, if the form is a relatively common one, the reader will be referred to a specific author or to an anthology where examples can be found. The entry ends with complete cross-references so that readers can discover relationships and similarities among many of the forms. It is my hope that users will find this edition even more useful than the original version of *The Book of Forms: A Handbook of Poetics*.

ACKNOWLEDGMENTS

The New Book of Forms is based upon these previous publications: *The Book of Forms*, New York: E. P. Dutton, copyright 1968 by Lewis Turco; *Creative Writing in Poetry*, Albany: State University of New York, copyright 1970 by the State University of New York; *Poetry: An Introduction Through Writing*, Reston, Virginia: Reston Publishing Company, copyright 1973 by Reston Publishing Company, Inc., a Prentice-Hall Company. All rights, including reversions of rights, reserved 1985, 1986 by Lewis Turco. Besides the acknowledgments previously made in these publications, the author owes a debt of gratitude to the State University of New York College at Oswego for a sabbatical leave during the spring term of 1986, when this book was put into its final shape.

The examples of Welsh poetry forms are reprinted from *The Airs of Wales: Medieval Welsh Poems in Modern English* by Wesli Court, published as a special issue of the Temple University *Poetry Newsletter*, No. 53, Fall 1981, all rights, including reversion of rights, reserved by Wesli Court, copyright 1981, 1986 by Wesli Court. "Love Curse," "Robyn and Makyn," and "The Eunuch Cat," are from *Courses in Laments*, Oswego: Mathom Publishing Co., copyright 1977 by Wesli Court. "Bref Double a l'Écho," "The Blacksmiths," "Hornpipepithalamion," "A Lover's Curse," and "The Swift Replies" are from *Curses and Laments*, published as a special issue of *Song*, No. 5, copyright 1978 by Richard Behm, all rights, including reversion of rights, reserved and copyrighted 1986 by Wesli Court. All rights to his other poems and to the remaining versions of the Medieval poems in modern English are reserved and copyrighted 1973, 1986 by Wesli Court.

The following poems are from an unpublished manuscript, *A Sampler of Hours: Poems on Lines from Emily Dickinson's Letters,* all rights reserved by Lewis Turco: "A Dainty Sum," originally published in *Poetry Northwest,* 1980; "First Snow," originally published as a Christmas card by George O'Connell and Lewis Turco, 1985; "The Naked Eye," originally published in *The Sewanee Review,* 1983; "Poetry" and "An Amherst Haiku," originally published in *The Ontario Review,* 1985. All other poems by Lewis Turco herein copyrighted 1960, 1971, 1973, 1980, 1981, 1986 by Lewis Turco.

Oswego, New York   L.T.
February 1986

1 A Handbook of Poetics

1 Introduction

Poetry is a literary GENRE or *type* of literature. Other genres are fiction, drama, and essay (among other kinds of "non-fiction" such as journalism, biography, autobiography, pedagogy, and so forth). Fiction can be defined as *written narrative;* drama, as *theatrical narrative;* and the essay, as *written rhetorical exposition.*

Fiction. All writers use language for various purposes, but in general the fiction writer's purpose is to tell a story; he or she thus uses language to carry a narrative. To tell a story the fiction writer needs four basic elements: *character, plot, atmosphere,* and *theme,* as well as a number of narrative language techniques. For further information about this genre, see the entry for NARRATIVES.

Drama. The dramatist's purpose, like that of the fiction writer, is to tell a story using character, plot, atmosphere, and theme; however, he or she can ordinarily use only the narrative language techniques of dialogue, monologue, or soliloquy. Unlike the fictionist, however, the dramatist can supplement these written narrative techniques with theatrical techniques such as representation (scenes, costumes, and physical actions). For further information about this genre, see the entry for DRAMATICS.

Essay. In its modern sense, an essay is a written discussion or exposition of a particular subject or an argument in favor of or against a point of view. In either case, the essayist has a point to make regarding a subject, and the focus is on the subject he or she is considering. The techniques of the essayist are generally rhetorical rather than narrative. The elements of an essay are likewise four: the *subject* being examined, the *thesis* or statement to be made concerning the subject, the *argument* or the logical proofs and data required to back the thesis statement, and the *conclusion* reached, which is usually identical with the thesis. For further information about this genre, see the entry on DIDACTICS.

Poetry. Since the poet can tell a story using either written or theatrical techniques, or can treat a particular subject by means of written rhetorical techniques, his or her primary focus must be on something other than the narrative or argument. In fact, what differentiates the poet from other writers is the *focus on mode,* on language itself. The poet focuses upon the literary resources of language in the same way a musician concentrates upon sound, the painter upon form, or the dancer upon movement.

Poetry can thus be defined as *the art of language,* as distinguished from fiction which is *the art of written narrative,* from drama, *the art of theatrical narrative,* or from the essay, *the art of written rhetoric.* The poet is specifically the artist of language; his or her concentration is upon the language itself. To concentrate upon the material of this genre, the poet, like the other writers, must utilize four elements, but in this case they are elements of language, on four different *levels,* rather than elements of narration or argument. The levels of poetry are the *typographical,* the *sonic,* the *sensory,* and the *ideational.* A fifth "level"—that of *fusion*—is a part of all genres. Fusion considers the question, "How do the elements of this story, poem, essay or play come together to achieve a final effect?"

2 The Typographical Level

Several things about a poem can be ascertained merely by looking at it on the printed page. First, one can generally tell in which of the two *modes* of language a poem is written; second, one can tell the *proportion in figure* of a poem; that is, whether it is written in *strophes* or *stanzas*.

Mode. There are only two modes in which any genre can be written, *prose* and *verse*. Prose is *unmetered* language; verse is *metered* language. Any of the genres can be written in either of the modes; that is, there are *prose narratives* and *verse narratives, prose dramas* and *verse dramas, prose essays* and *verse essays*. Likewise, there are *prose poems* and *verse poems*. Depending upon the poet's culture, a poem can be written primarily in prose, as in the Hebrew Old Testament, or in verse, as in the Anglo-Saxon poem, *Beowulf.* There is, thus, only one logical answer to the question, "What is the difference between poetry and prose?" *Poetry is a genre, and verse is a mode.*

On the typographical level, it is usually possible to distinguish, from the lengths of the lines, whether a poem is written in prose or verse. Prose poems generally have lines of various lengths; verse poems ordinarily show lines of similar length. Sight, however, is not always accurate, and lines ought to be *scanned* to discover whether or not *meter* is present.

To meter means to count. In verse, what is usually counted is syllables—all syllables, only stressed syllables, or all syllables *and* stressed syllables. Meters will be further explained when I discuss the sonic level of poetry. *To scan* means to as-

5

certain the number of syllables in a verse-mode poem. Scansion will also be discussed later.

Sometimes an entire poem will be built primarily upon the typographical level of language. Such poems are called *spatials,* and they achieve their primary effect on the level of sight. There are two kinds of spatial poetry, the *calligramme,* an otherwise normal poem written in a shaped stanza, and the *concrete poem,* which achieves its effect mainly through its configuration. For more information about such poems, see the entry on SPATIALS.

Proportion in Figure. A poem can be written in sections and even in subsections. Larger sections are called "cantos," "fits," "movements," or other terms. Smaller sections are either *strophes* or *stanzas.* Stanzas are short sections of a single poem, each made up of the same number of lines. Strophes are short sections of a single poem made up of differing numbers of lines.

Various other things can be discerned simply by studying the appearance of a poem, aspects having to do with *layout* and *punctuation.* Prose poems are sometimes mislabeled "free verse," but this misnomer is a contradiction in terms, as we have seen, for there are only two modes of language—prose and verse. Either language is metered, or it is not metered; it cannot be both simultaneously. If language is not metered, it is prose; however, prose poems are sometimes laid out on the page so that they appear to approximate verse.

Longer-lined prose poems are often laid out by the sentence, printed on the page as a visible unit rather than as part of a paragraph. This practice was used by the eighteenth-century English poet Christopher Smart and the nineteenth-century American poet Walt Whitman in their prose poems. Such works are often built on a system of grammatic parallels (to be discussed later). Poems constructed on this principle can often be easily distinguished by running your eye down the left-hand margin of the poem. You are likely to discover that each line begins with the same word or phrase—again, such as in the work of Smart, Whitman, Carl Sandburg, Robinson Jeffers, and many poets of the twentieth century. Shorter-lined prose poems are often laid out by the clause or the phrase, each clause or phrase being allocated its own line. This construct is called *line-phrasing,* and it occasionally omits punctuation at the ends of lines entirely, the end of the line serving as *sight punctuation.* See the entry on the TRIVERSEN for further discussion of line-phrasing.

Verse poems might exhibit *end-stopping,* which means there is terminal punctuation—an exclamation point, a question mark, or a period—at the end of a line ("stich" in older English terminology) or of a larger unit such as a couplet ("twime"), triplet ("thrime"), or quatrain ("tetrastich"). If there is no punctuation and the line runs onto the next line, the poem is *enjambed.* A *verse paragraph* may or may not coincide with a stanza or a strophe. Like the prose paragraph, the verse paragraph is a group of lines in a metrical poem that deals with matters that have logical relationships with one another and a common focus. If the verse paragraph does not coincide with the end of a stanza or a strophe, the poet will often drop down a step typographically within a line to indicate that a new paragraph is beginning. The device of *stepping* is also sometimes used to indicate a caesura, or a pause in the *center* of a line. Rather than stepping the line, a poet might, on occasion, use sight punctuation in the form of an extra space within a line to indicate the caesura. More will be said about the caesura in the chapter "The Sonic Level" and in the entry ANGLO-SAXON PROSODY.

3 The Sonic Level

Rhythm is at the root of traditional English-language poetry, and one of the basic functions of the poet is to *order the rhythms of language*. Several terms must be distinguished here:

1. *Cadence* is the alternation of stressed and unstressed syllables in language.
2. *Rhythm* is the movement of cadences in language.
3. *Prosody* is a system of poetic composition.
4. *Meter* is a particular pattern of prosody that counts syllables in verse.

PROSE PROSODIES

The oldest prosody in the world is based not upon counting syllables, but on grammatically parallel language structures. The theory of *grammatic parallelism* is simple: within a sentence or longer unit, *repeat the same grammatical structures;* for instance, "I came, I saw, I conquered." This line is one sentence made up of three independent clauses. All the subjects are the same; all the predicates are in the same verb tense. If the clauses are broken into lines, the parallels are immediately apparent:

I came,
I saw,
I conquered.

Let us look at another sentence: "I like bananas, cherries, and apples."

subject	transitive verb	object
I	like	bananas
		cherries
		apples

The compound object is in parallel. Though parallelism can get a great deal more complicated than this, the principle is always the same. Parallel structures appear in both prose and verse, but as a governing prosody or *system* of poetry composition, it appears most often in prose.

By repeating parallel structures, the poet causes stressed and unstressed syllables to appear in approximately, sometimes exactly, the same places, thus setting up a *rhythm*. Here is an example, a portion of The Song of Solomon from the King James Version of the Bible:

Behold, thou art fair, my love; behold, thou art fair; thou hast doves' eyes within thy locks: thy hair is as a flock of goats, that appear from mount Gilead.

Thy teeth are like a flock of sheep that are even shorn, which came up from the washing; whereof every one bears twins, and none is barren among them.

Thy lips are like a thread of scarlet, and thy speech is comely: thy temples are like a piece of pomegranate within thy locks.

Thy neck is like the tower of David builded for an armoury, whereon there hang a thousand bucklers, all shields of mighty men.

Thy two breasts are like two young roes that are twins, which feed among the lilies.

Notice that, in this example, a certain rhythm is set up by the repetitions of the parallel structures in the first two lines:

Behŏld, thŏu ărt fáir, mў lóve;

bĕhóld, thŏu ărt fáir;

thŏu hăst dóves' éyes

withĭn thў lócks:

thy̆ háir ĭs ás ă flŏck ŏf góats,

thăt ăppéar frŏm Móunt Gílĕad.

Several things have been changed in this passage. First, it has been *line-phrased;* second, it has been scanned—an *ictus* or accent-mark (ʹ) has been placed above each stressed syllable and a *breve* (˘) above each unstressed syllable. The following shows the rhythmic patterns created by the parallel structures of the first two lines:

˘ʹ ˘˘ʹ ˘ʹ

˘ʹ ˘˘ʹ

Though this example is prose, not verse, it can be seen that the repetition of parallel grammatical structures produces an effect *like* that of verse, and even the typographical appearance of verse can be reproduced by line-phrasing. You can also divide these rhythmic patterns from one another by the use of dividers:

˘ʹ|˘˘ʹ|˘ʹ

˘ʹ|˘˘

The first pattern contains two syllables, the first unaccented and the second accented. This pattern is commonly called an *iamb.* The second pattern has three syllables, two unaccented followed by an accented syllable. Such a pattern is commonly called an *anapest.* More will be said later about these patterns, called *verse feet,* when I speak of meters. For the moment, it is sufficient to understand that *English prose rhythms are predominantly iambic and anapestic.*

To return to grammatic parallelism, there are four major types of specific parallel structures found in the Bible: *synonymous, synthetic, antithetical,* and *climactic.*

Synonymous parallelism breaks each clause or sentence in two. The second half paraphrases the statement made in the first half:

For, lo, the winter is past,   the rain is over and gone;
The flowers appear on the earth;   the time of the singing
   of birds is come, and the voice of the turtle is heard in
   the land.

Synthetic parallelism also divides the clause or sentence, but the second half gives a consequence of the first half:

I rose up to open to my beloved;   and my hands dropped
   with myrrh, and my fingers with sweet smelling myrrh,
   upon the handles of the lock.

Antithetical parallelism, too, breaks the clause or sentence in half, but the second half rebuts or contradicts the first half:

I sleep,   but my heart waketh. . . .

Climactic parallelism does not necessarily break a clause or sentence in half; rather, it can pile stronger and stronger clauses or sentences upon one another until the series ends at its apex:

Awake, O north wind; and come, thou south; blow upon my
   garden, that the spices thereof may flow out. Let my beloved
   come into his garden, and eat his pleasant fruits.

This type of "heaping figure" is also called a *catalog*.

ISOVERBAL* PROSODY

In Hebrew poetry, other strictures might be imposed upon the system of grammatics. For instance, a *perfect parallel (isocolon)* not only observes the requirements of divided parallel structures, but also might require the same number of words in each half, or even the same number of syllables. Here is an example drawn from Psalm 26—in these lines the word count in each half-sentence is seven (7):

$$\overset{1}{}\overset{2}{}\overset{3}{}\quad\overset{4}{}\overset{5}{}\quad\overset{6}{}\quad\overset{7}{}\quad\overset{1}{}\quad\overset{2}{}\overset{3}{}\quad\overset{4}{}$$
For thy lovingkindness is before mine eyes: and I have walked
$$\overset{5}{}\overset{6}{}\quad\overset{7}{}$$
in thy truth.

*A term coined by Dr. Sally M. Gall to replace the term *wordcount*.

1 2   3   4   5   6   7   1   2   34   5   6
I have not sat with vain persons,   neither will I go in with
7
dissemblers.
1   3   4   5   6 7   1   2   3   4
I have hated the congregation of evildoers;   and will not sit
5   6   7
with the wicked.

Isoverbal prosody can be used by itself as a loose *metrical* system; strictly speaking, however, only syllable-counting systems are truly metrical. The effect of isoverbal prosody is more like that of prose, since words can contain various numbers of syllables.

There are three specific isoverbal prosodies:

1. *Normative wordcount* assigns the same number of words to each line, as in the example above.

2. *Quantitative wordcount* varies the lengths of lines in the first stanza, but the following stanzas keep the same word counts as the first, line for line.

3. *Variable wordcount* sets certain limits on the lengths of lines, but within these limits the number of words per line can vary—for instance, the poet might decide that there will be a minimum of three words in each line and a maximum of seven.

METRICAL PROSODIES

SYLLABIC PROSODY

This system is based upon counting all syllables in a line of verse, whether they are stressed or unstressed. Japanese verse is syllabic, and, more to the point, so is Celtic verse—the poetry of the ancient Gaels of Scotland, Ireland, Wales, Cornwall, and other regions of the British Isles. Furthermore, French prosody is syllabic. The latter, introduced into England proper at the time of the Norman Invasion (A.D. 1066) is thus ancient and native to English literature. There is even an American verse form based upon syllabics—see the entry on the CINQUAIN.

There are three specific syllabic prosodies:

1. *Normative syllabics* assigns the same number of syllables to each line.

2. *Quantitative syllabics* varies the lengths of lines in the first stanza, but the following stanzas keep the same syllable counts as the first, line for line.

3. *Variable syllabics* sets certain limits for the lengths of lines, but within these limits the number of syllables per line can vary—for instance, the poet might decide that there will be a minimum of three syllables in each line and a maximum of seven.

Here is a normative syllabic poem, each line having six (6) syllables. It is a composite poem based on lines from Emily Dickinson's letters:

A Dainty Sum
1   2 3   4 5   6
One is a dainty sum!
1   2   3   4   5   6
One bird, one cage, one flight;
1   2   3   4   5   6
one song in those far woods

where mandrake likes to dream,
where dragonfly patrols
its image in the stream;

one song out of the limb
of juniper or fir
moving across the field

where primrose tries to snare
the note of solitude,
the message from the air.

The following is a quantitative syllabic poem from the same source. The syllable counts are 8–7–8:

First Snow
A thousand little winds wafted
    to me this morning an air
fragrant with forest leaves and bright

autumnal berries. Now and then
a gray leaf fell. Crickets sang
all day long. High in a crimson

tree a belated bird trembled—
there must be many moments
in an eternal day. Alas!

I remember the leaves were falling,
and now there are falling snows.
Are not leaves the brethren of snows?

I dream of being a grandame
and binding my silver hairs,
the children dancing around me.

These poems are examples of *found* poetry, or at least partially found. Sometimes in reading you run across a piece of prose you feel is "poetic"—that is, it is written in enhanced language. In fact, it is poetry, despite its being written in the prose mode. Because of tradition, English readers think poetry must be written in verse. If we cannot get over our mind-set, or if we want to call other people's attention to our discovery, we might set the lines off to look like verse or, in fact, put them *in* verse (as in the preceding poems). Found poetry is a *subgenre* of the literary genre called poetry; subgenres will be discussed more fully elsewhere.

Lines of syllabic verse can be described by affixing these prefixes to the root "syllabics": mono (1), di (2), tri (3), tetra (4), penta (5), hexa (6), hepta (7), octo (8), nono (9), deca (10), and hendeca (11). The poem "A Dainty Sum," then, is written in hexasyllabic lines. The first and third lines of each triplet stanza of "First Snow" are octosyllabic, but the second lines are heptasyllabic. (Note that the shorter lines are indented.)

ACCENTUAL PROSODY

This system is based upon counting only those syllables that are stressed—there can be any number of unstressed syllables in a line. Old English (Anglo-Saxon) prosody is in fact a *specific form* of accentual verse. The oldest European vernacular literature (that is, literature other than classical Latin or Greek) is written in accentual prosody, which is ancient and native to England.

There are several specific accentual prosodies:

1. *Normative accentuals* assigns the same number of stresses to each line: see the entry on ANGLO-SAXON PROSODY.

2. *Quantitative accentuals* varies the lengths of lines in the first stanza, but the following stanzas keep the same stress counts as the first, line for line (as in SONG MEASURE found in the entry titled EDDA MEASURES).

3. *Variable accentuals* sets certain limits for the lengths of lines, but within these limits the number of stresses per line can vary, as in the entries on TRIVERSEN and TRIVERSEN STANZA.

The words *stress* and *accent* are often used interchangeably, but we can differentiate them by thinking of stress as emphasis placed upon a syllable by special means, as in rhetorical stress: "*What* did you say?" Accent is simply the ordinary emphasis placed on at least one syllable in a word of two or more syllables. To find out which syllable of a word is normally accented, a dictionary can, and *should,* be consulted. Words of one syllable might or might not be stressed, depending on their importance or on their context in the sentence. Coordinating conjunctions (and, but, or, nor, for), articles (a, the), prepositions (of, on, in), and such parts of speech are seldom stressed. On the other hand, verbs and nouns of one syllable are often stressed.

English does not easily accommodate three unstressed syllables in a row; therefore, when three normally unstressed syllables appear together, the middle syllable is *promoted* to stressed status:

Weakly it was running in the road.

Notice that a dot was placed over the promoted syllables in this line. This mark indicates a *secondary* or weaker stress.

Linguists differentiate among several levels of stress: primary, secondary, tertiary, quaternary, and so forth. For our purposes, however, we need be concerned only with overstressing or *sprung* stress, ordinary stress, and secondary stress.

Much accentual verse, and some syllabic verse—especially Celtic syllabic verse—is written alliteratively: the stressed syllables are overemphasized or sprung by a series of words that use the same beginning consonantal sound, as in "*L*ooms as the *l*ast *l*augh at *l*ast. . . ." If we scan this line we will discover that the stresses fall on the alliterated first syllables:

*L*óoms as the *l*ást *l*áugh at *l*ást

(Note that the accent mark is always placed above the vowel sound, not the consonant.)

If we listen closely to the line, we will also hear that it tends to divide itself in half—there is a pause in the line between the second and third accented syllables:

*L*óoms as the *l*ást · *l*áugh at *l*ást

This method is that of ANGLO-SAXON PROSODY and of some of the EDDA MEASURES: four stressed syllables in a *stich*. Some of the stressed syllables will be *sprung* with alliteration, assonance, rhyme, or vocalic and consonantal echo, all of which will be discussed later. The stich is broken into *hemistichs* (half-lines) by a *caesura* in the center of the line. In a whole stich there are four stresses; in the hemistichs, two stresses (*dipods*).

1. The two center-stressed syllables can alliterate:

óver the *s*társ · *s*túnning their fíres.

2. The first three stressed syllables can alliterate:

But the *l*éaf shall *l*íe · *l*íghtly upón him.

3. The last three stressed syllables can alliterate:

its únique *s*ýmmetry · the *s*úmmit of *s*óng.

4. All four syllables can alliterate, as in the previously quoted line ("Looms as the last laugh at last").

5. Sometimes the alliteration continues into the following stich, and sometimes there is cross-alliteration between stichs:

his b*l*óod *spr*ínging · from *r*ínging *r*óck

till the *l*óng *r*áin · of tíme shall *sp*íll. . . .

6. On occasion, what is alliterated is the *absence* of consonants; then, any vowel can alliterate (actually, *consonate*) with any other:

*á*t this mártyr · and *á*t his *á*rt.

(Note that in this last example the vowel sounds "at" and "martyr," and "at" and "art" are not the same.)

H. Idris Bell and David Bell, in their translation of the medieval Welsh poet Dafydd ap Gwilym (*Fifty Poems,* London, 1942), describe the bardic sonic devices, known as *cynghanedd* (kíng-ha-neth), that are associated with medieval Welsh syllabic verse but whose effects are similar to those found in association with Anglo-Saxon prosody. There are four main types of cynghanedd:

1. "In *Cynghanedd Groes* there is an exact correspondence between the consonants in the first half of the line and those in the second, so that every consonant in the first finds its [consonantal echo] in the second, and there is no consonant unaccounted for in the scheme, with the exception of the final syllable in each half":

1   2 3 4   5   1   2 3 4   5
This tone is his, · the stone's song, . . .

2. "In *Cynghanedd Draws* the same system is apparent, except that there is, as it were, an island in the centre of the line in which the consonants are in isolation and are not echoed elsewhere":

1   2 3 4 5 6   7   1 2 3   4 5 6 7
He is life's fool, · and his leaf's fall. . . .

3. "In *Cynghanedd Lusg* the penultimate (next-to-last) stressed syllable is rhymed with a syllable in the first part of the line":

his blóod *sprúng* · from *rúng* róck. . . .

4. ". . . and *Cynghanedd Sain* has an internal rhyme together with [consonantal echo] between the second rhyming word and the last word in the line":

nó *óther* than · *bróther* of his bréath, . . .

Twentieth-century Welsh poets such as Dylan Thomas have used cynghanedd effects in their poetry, though they have not necessarily followed the exact strictures of these four patterns. All these lines, however, were taken from a single poem, which itself is an illustration of how various alliterative and echoic devices can work when they are put together. Notice that, in this poem, the lines have been *stepped* at the caesurae:

The Morbid Man Singing

This tone is his,
          the stone's song,
No other than
          brother of his breath,
fang of water,
          tongue of the air.
He is life's fool,
          and his leaf's fall
looms as the last
          laugh at last
at this martyr
          and at his art.
But the leaf shall lie
          lightly upon him,
its unique symmetry
          the summit of song
which he will enter
          leaf-fall and winter—

his blood sprung
   from rung rock
till the long rain
   of time shall spill
over the stars,
   stunning their fires.
     —WESLI COURT

If all syllables in each line are counted, the numbers will be seen to vary, while the number of accented syllables remains constant. *Whatever remains most constant is the poem's prosody.* For another example of normative accentual verse, see the entry on the BOB AND WHEEL.

Gerard Manley Hopkins in his poem "God's Grandeur" paid no attention to keeping only a certain number of beats to the line, but he heavily accented his stresses. Although the following poem is rhymed like an ITALIAN SONNET, ordinarily written in iambic pentameter, accentual-syllabic verse (to be discussed subsequently), it is actually an example of allit-erated, *variable accentual verse.* Hopkins called this system "sprung rhythm." The principle is much the same as in Anglo-Saxon prosody, except that there can be more or fewer than four accents in the line, and Hopkins used rhyme as well as alliteration. Note that the rhyme scheme deter-mines the line indentations:

God's Grandeur

The wórld is chárged with the grándeur of Gód.

 It will fláme óut, like shíning from shóok foíl;

 It gáthers to a greátness, líke the óoze of oíl

Crúshed. Whý do mén then nów not réck his ród?
Generations have trod, have trod, have trod;
 And all is seared with trade; bleared, smeared with toil;
 And wears man's smudge and shares man's smell: the soil
Is bare now, nor can foot feel, being shod.

And for all this, nature is never spent;
  There lives the dearest freshness deep down things;
And though the last lights off the black West went
  Oh, morning, at the brown brink eastward, springs—
Because the Holy Ghost over the bent
  World broods with warm breast and with ah! bright wings.
                                    —GERARD MANLEY HOPKINS

Notice in particular line four, which contains eight stresses in a row, impossible in English without overstressing by using sonic devices such as rhyme (men-then), alliteration (now-not, reck-rod), consonantal echo (me*n*-the*n*-*n*ow-*n*ot), or assonance (m*e*n-th*e*n-r*e*ck). Note also that, despite overstressing, the accents on "do," "then," and "not" are secondary. Instead of the situation where the central syllable in a row of three unstressed syllables is promoted to secondary stress, here the central syllable in a row of three stressed syllables is *demoted* to secondary stress.

A schematic diagram of the scansion of line four, if each syllable is represented by the letter X, would look like this:

´   ´ ˙ ´   ˙ ´ ˙ ´   ´
x   x x x   x x x x   x x
Crushed. Why do men then now not reck his rod?

If we remove the words,

´ ´ ´ ˙ ˙ ´ ˙ ´   ´
x x x x x x x x x x

An American form of variable accentuals is called TRIVERSEN stanza, and it has been widely used in the twentieth century. Based partly on grammatics, partly on unalliterated accentual verse, the triversen was the favorite form, and the invention, of William Carlos Williams.

PODIC PROSODY

Podics stands halfway between strong-stress verse and accentual-syllabic prosody; in fact, because it typically uses rhyme, many people believe it is accentual-syllabics. Podics is a holdover in folk poetry—ballads, nursery rhymes, broadside verse—of the old Anglo-Saxon line.

The meter of a podic poem (or of any accentual verses) is indicated by affixing the standard prefixes to the root *pod,* which means "foot" (although the meters of podic prosody are not verse feet in the normal sense of the term used in English poetics). Thus, "monopodic" means one-stress, "dipodic," two-stress, and so on through tripodic, tetrapodic, pentapodic, hexapodic, and so forth. The primary meter of podic verse is *dipody*.

The dipodic line, like the hemistich of Anglo-Saxon prosody, contains two accented syllables. *Strong stresses* only are counted; unstressed and secondary-stressed syllables are generally ignored in the metric. Each line containing two strong stresses is, in effect, a hemistich of Anglo-Saxon prosody:

Old Mother Goose, · When she wanted to wander,

Rode through the air · On a very fine gander.

Note that the normally stressed first syllable in "Mother" has been demoted to secondary stress because of the sprung, long $\bar{o}$ sound in "Old" and the even heavier long $\overline{oo}$ sound in "Goose." Normally, two dipodic lines (one stich) form a *half-unit* of dipodic verse, and two more hemistichs (again, one stich) are needed to complete the couplet unit (*distich* or *twime*), which is rhymed—often with falling rhymes (feminine endings—further explained later under the heading "Proportion in Rhyme").

Put as simply as possible, a dipodic unit is nothing more than a couplet made of two rhyming stichs (a distich) of Anglo-Saxon prosody. The caesura between hemistichs becomes the ends of lines 1 and 3, so that the couplet appears on paper as a quatrain:

Old Mother Goose,
When she wanted to wander,

Rode through the air
On a very fine gander.
            —ANONYMOUS

A whole set of stanzas in the family called COMMON MEA-
SURE and BALLAD STANZA grew out of this podic quatrain.
Many hymns are cast in common measure forms. Emily
Dickinson, Isaac Watts, and William Blake, among many
others, used common measure forms, often regularized as
accentual-syllabics rather than podics.

Although podics added rhyme and did not necessarily
keep the alliteration of Anglo-Saxon prosody, especially not
in every line, the verse did depend heavily on sonic devices.
J. R. R. Tolkien, in his "Prefatory Remarks" to J. P. Clark's
translation of *Beowulf* (London, 1941), isolated six basic
hemistichs in Anglo-Saxon prosody, and these basic half-
lines have been retained in many dipodic poems:

1. The *double-fall* (ˊ ◡ ˊ ◡), as in

Mistress Mary,

Quite contrary

2. The *double-rise* (◡ ˊ ◡ ˊ), as in

With silver bells

and cockle shells

3. The *rise-and-fall* (◡ ˊ ˊ ◡), as in

The two gray kits

4. The *rise-and-descend* (ˊ ˊ · ◡), as in

My Maid Mary

5. The *fall-and-ascend* (ˊ ˊ ◡ ˊ), as in

To woo the owl

6. The *descend-and-rise* (ˊˊ˘ˊ), as in

Hárk! Hárk! thĕ lárk!

There are, however, many more rhythmic variations possible. Two others are also quite common:

7. The *short rocking foot* (ˊ˘ˊ), as in

Sée thĕm júmp úp ănd dówn!

(Called the *amphimacer* in accentual-syllabic verse, it is almost never found in English language poetry written in that prosody.)

8. The *long rocking foot* (ˊ˘˘ˊ), as in

Híppĕty-hóp, híppĕty hóp!

9. The *long rise* (˘˘ˊˊ), as in

Ănd ă óne-twó, ănd ă thrée-fóur!

(Harvey Gross in his book *Sound and Form in Modern Poetry* [Ann Arbor, 1968] calls this rhythm the *double iamb* and discovers it frequently in accentual-syllabic verse, where it substitutes for two iambic feet. Robert Frost used it often in his work—see "Mending Wall" below.)

Skeltonics, or "tumbling verse," is insistently rhymed dipodics. Turn to John Skelton's "Justice Now" in the entry on SATIRICS for an example. A scansion of the poem reveals a number of Tolkien's hemistichs. A much more sophisticated use of podic prosody can be illustrated by the first stanza of the following poem:

Bells for John Whiteside's Daughter
Thĕre wăs súch spéed · ĭn hĕr líttlĕ bódў,

Ănd súch líghtness · ĭn hĕr fóotfáll,

Ĭt ĭs nó wóndĕr · hĕr brówn stúdў

Ăstónĭshĕs · ŭs áll.
—JOHN CROWE RANSOM

This poem is an ELEGY. The first three lines of the stanza are dipodic because there is a caesura in each line; otherwise, the lines would be tetrapodic. The fourth line of each quatrain is tripodic, so this poem is of mixed line-lengths. Note the long rises in the first and fourth hemistichs, the rise-and-fall in the sixth, the promotion of the central unstressed syllable in the first tripod. It is quite possible for a poet to mix podic line-lengths in a poem—Skelton often does it in his tumbling verse. If there were not a preponderance of dipods in Skelton's verse, the specific prosody would have to be called *variable podics* (perhaps it ought to be called so anyway).

ACCENTUAL-SYLLABIC PROSODY

This metrical system counts both the number of stressed syllables in the line *and* the number of unstressed syllables in the same line. Moreover, the stressed syllables alternate *more or less* regularly in the line of verse to create *verse feet,* which are also counted. There are three specific accentual-syllabic prosodies: (1) normative, (2) quantitative, and (3) variable.

Normative accentual-syllabics have a *running foot* (with variations), a predominating verse foot in the lines of a poem, each of those lines containing the same number of feet. The symbols indicating the *breve* ($\smile$) and the *ictus* ($\prime$) have already been discussed. The *macron* (–) is the same as the ictus and, like it, is placed above the stressed vowel. The symbol for the *secondary stress* ($\cdot$) appears over the stressed vowel; the *caesura* ($\cdot$) appears in the *center* of the line (in accentual-syllabic verse of four to six feet, after the second or third verse foot). The *foot divider* (||) separates verse feet. All these marks have been used previously, but one other must be explained: the virgule (/) is a stroke used to separate *verses* when they are written out like prose, *not* to separate verse feet:

O my luve's like · a red, red rose, / That's newly sprung in June; /

O, my luve's like · the melodie / That's sweetly played in tune.

—ROBERT BURNS

In this passage, the stress on "O" is secondary, perhaps not even a stress at all in comparison with the springing of "luve's like" and "red, red rose." Even the second "red" is demoted because of its position as the central syllable in a series of three stressed syllables. The effect of these four lines, then, is:

lines	meters and rhymes
1.	˘ ʊ′ ′ ʊ′ ˘ ′ x x x x x x x a
2.	ʊ′ ʊ′ ʊ′ x x x x x b
3.	˘ ʊ′ ′ ʊ′ ʊ′ x x x x x x x c
4.	ʊ′ ʊ′ ʊ′ x x x x x b

In this schematic diagram, the rhyme scheme of the first quatrain stanza is shown, but the caesurae have been taken out. The effect of this passage is somewhat podic, but a count of the syllables will show that lines one (1) and three (3) contain exactly eight syllables, and that lines two (2) and four (4) contain exactly six. Furthermore, a recurring stress pattern is evident in the corresponding lines (one and three: ˙ʊ′ʊ′ʊ′; two and four: ʊ′ʊ′ʊ′). The predominating foot, therefore, is an *iamb*. All three elements are thus regular—syllable count in a line, number of stressed syllables in a line, and number and kind of verse feet in a line.

There are four standard verse feet in English prosody:

1. The *iamb* is a verse foot of two syllables, only the second being stressed: ʊ′.
2. The *anapest* has three syllables, only the third of which is stressed: ʊʊ′.
3. The *trochee* consists of two syllables, but the stress pattern of the iamb is reversed: ′ʊ.
4. The *dactyl* is made of three syllables, but the stress pattern of the anapest is reversed: ′ʊʊ.

There are several minor verse feet in English prosody, usually used as variations only:

5. The *headless iamb* is a foot of one stressed syllable, as is the

6. *tailless trochee:* ʹ. One can tell these two feet apart only from their position in a line of verse. They occur, for instance, when the unstressed first syllable of an iamb is dropped as a variation in a line of verse, or when the unstressed second syllable of a trochee is dropped for the same reason.

7. The *spondee* is a foot of two syllables, both of which are stressed: ʹ ʹ.

8. The *amphibrach* is a foot of three syllables, only the second of which is stressed: ᴜ ʹ ᴜ.

9. The *double iamb* is a foot of four syllables, the first two unstressed and the second two stressed: ᴜ ᴜ ʹ ʹ. It equals two iambs in a line of verse.

Classical prosodists would say that the double iamb is a combination of two feet, the pyrrhic (ᴜ ᴜ) and the spondee. The pyrrhic, however, does not seem to appear elsewhere in English prosody, unless as a variation in a trochaic poem that reverses the double iamb (ʹ ʹ ᴜ ᴜ), which would substitute for two trochees and perhaps best be called a *double trochee*.

Other classical feet do not apply to English prosody. An *amphimacer* (ʹ ᴜ ʹ) is either a headless iamb and an iamb, or a trochee and a tailless trochee. We know that the *tribrach* (ᴜ ᴜ ᴜ), three unstressed syllables, cannot exist, for the middle syllable would be promoted. The reverse occurs in the case of the *molossus* (ʹ ʹ ʹ), for the central syllable is demoted. The *bacchic* (ᴜ ʹ ʹ) would be an iamb and a tailless trochee, and the *antibacchic* (ʹ ʹ ᴜ) is a headless iamb and a trochee.

Variations in a line of English verse are important, for in normative accentual-syllabic verse, it is variation against the pattern, and not strict adherence to the pattern, that satisfies the ear. The poetaster (an unskilled versifier) memorizes a pattern and works with it, whereas the poet understands a pattern and works against it. Regularity of meter is uninteresting; *counterpoint*—rhythm against the normative beat—is interesting. On the other hand, too much variation is disconcerting and awkward.

The name of the predominating foot, plus the standard prefixes attached to the root "meter," identify the metric of normative accentual-syllabics. For instance, the word "iambic" plus "monometer" indicates that the length of the line is one (1) foot; trochaic dimeter equals two (2) feet; anapestic trimeter equals three (3) feet; dactylic tetrameter equals four (4) feet; iambic pentameter equals five (5) feet, and so forth. This last line, iambic pentameter, is the HEROIC LINE of English poetry. Any poem written in this line is HEROIC VERSE, whether rhymed or unrhymed (see HEROICS).

The term *blank* merely means *unrhymed metered verse*. If *any* line of accentual-syllabic verse is unrhymed, it is called BLANK VERSE; however, this term usually is understood to mean the iambic pentameter line, unless some other normative meter is specified. The terms *blank verse* and *free verse* are often confused with one another. Free verse is either prose or some unidentified prosody, such as variable accentuals, and both can rhyme. The twentieth-century poet Ogden Nash made a career of writing rhymed prose poems. *Blank verse cannot rhyme.*

Scansion is extremely important in accentual-syllabic verse. Scansion describes a norm, not an absolute. *Some* lines of a particular iambic pentameter poem, for instance, might not contain a single iamb, but *most will.* Moreover, in most lines iambs will predominate. The first four lines of Robert Frost's "Mending Wall" will serve as an example:

> Something there is that doesn't love a wall,
> That sends the frozen-ground-swell under it,
> And spills the upper boulders in the sun,
> And makes gaps even two can pass abreast.

The verse should be read *naturally,* like prose, letting the accents fall as they will. *Regular meters should not be forced upon the lines.* Furthermore, the poem should be read in sentences, not by the line—there should be no pause at the end of a line unless there is punctuation. Punctuation, wherever it appears in verse, should be responded to just as in prose.

After you have read the Frost poem aloud, listening to yourself as you speak, the lines can be scanned by putting ictus marks or secondary stress dots over those syllables that sound heavier than the others:

Something there is that doesn't love a wall,

That sends the frozen-ground-swell under it,

And spills the upper boulders in the sun,

And makes gaps even two can pass abreast.

After this task has been done, the breve marks can be added over the rest of the syllables:

Something there is that doesn't love a wall,

That sends the frozen-ground-swell under it,

And spills the upper boulders in the sun,

And makes gaps even two can pass abreast.

When the scansion marks are isolated, the pattern looks like this:

    ⏑⏑⏑⏑⏑⏑⏑⏑⏑⏑
    ⏑⏑⏑⏑⏑⏑·⏑·
    ⏑⏑⏑⏑⏑⏑·⏑⏑
    ⏑⏑··⏑⏑⏑⏑⏑

This pattern shows the kind of foot that predominates (⏑´), and if you count the syllables in each line, the norm will be ten, or, in the first line,

    ´⏑⏑´⏑´⏑´⏑´
    x x x x x x x x x x

Now you can divide the verse feet, one from the other:

    ´⏑|⏑´|⏑´|⏑´|⏑´

The predominant foot is iambic, so the verse is an iambic poem. There are five feet in a line, therefore it is an iambic pentameter poem. Furthermore, it is unrhymed—an iambic pentameter, blank verse poem.

In line one (1) of the Frost poem, a trochee has been substituted for an iamb in the first foot. In line two (2), there is a demotion in the first syllable of the fourth foot and a secondary stress substituted for the normal stress in the fifth foot. Line three (3) contains a promotion in the second syllable of the fourth foot, and in line four (4), a trochee has been substituted for an iamb in the second foot. Also in this latter foot, a secondary stress stands in place of the unaccented syllable of the trochee (a "descend," as in podic prosody).

Although one reader's scansion of this poem may differ from another's, all readers will agree that the normative meter is iambic and that the length of the line is pentameter. Pronunciation, including stressing, varies from region to region, and individuals tend to put more rhetorical emphasis on certain words; nevertheless, anyone with a trained ear will hear the running foot.

The rest of Frost's poem will illustrate many of the other types of variation possible; for instance, line eleven (11) begins with a double iamb:

But at spring mending-time we find them there.

Systems of variation are called *counterpoint*. The term *acatalexis* designates a perfect line of accentual-syllabic verse. For instance, in an iambic tetrameter poem, an acatalectic line will have eight syllables and four stresses, the unaccented syllables alternating regularly with the accented syllables:

"I love your hair that way," she said.

This example, and those following, are taken from a single poem whose normative meter is iambic tetrameter.

A line is made *catalectic* by dropping a syllable from the end of the line:

corrupting mem*ories* of childhood

If the dropped syllable is one that is stressed, the line will normally be shortened—producing a trimeter line. If the dropped syllable is unstressed, the line is not shortened (see the previously mentioned tailless trochee). Note the elision in "memories"—pronounced *mem'ries* (elision will be discussed later).

Dropping more than one syllable at the end of the line makes it *brachycatalectic*. A line is made *hypercatalectic* by adding a syllable at the end of the line:

Though minds have likened worlds to stages, . . .

If the syllable added is stressed, the line will be lengthened, *unless the stressed syllable is part of a spondaic foot (′′).*

A line is made *acephalous* (headless) by dropping unstressed syllables from the beginning of the line (see the headless iamb discussed previously):

dampening our solitude, . . .

A line is made anacrustic by adding unaccented syllables to the beginning of the line:

and of youth must come at last to tatters.

In effect, an anapest has been substituted for an iamb in the first foot. Notice that this line is both anacrustic and hypercatalectic.

Quality refers to the substitution of one kind of verse foot for another; specifically, the substitution of a verse foot that differs from the normative meter of the line:

no game's a turn that r*eally* matters.

In this line, a spondee has been substituted for the normative iamb in the first foot, and an amphibrach for the normative iamb in the last foot. Adding the stressed syllable as part of the spondee has not lengthened the line, nor has the meter of the line been changed through hypercatalexis. Notice the *y-glide* elision in r*e*ally.

In English verse lines of four beats or longer, a *natural caesura*—only a brief hesitation—occurs often after the second or third stressed syllable:

We sought through rooms · for something warm. . . .

Qualitative caesura is caused by manipulating measures through substitution:

Mutually grappled, · we ate the fruit—

Notice the substitution of a dactyl for the normative iamb in the first foot, and of a trochee in the second foot. The normative meter resumes in the third foot, and the caesura occurs where two unaccented syllables come together. Note the *w-glide* elision in mut*ua*lly.

Punctuational caesura is caused by punctuation placed somewhere in the center of the line to indicate phrasing:

its skin and core—and quaffed flesh deeply, . . .

Compensatory caesura occurs when the caesura compensates for a missing syllable dropped from the center of a line:

corrupting memories⌐⌐ of childhood, . . .

Compensation occurs when a missing half-foot or larger unit in one line is made up for with an extra unit added to the same line or to a preceding or following line:

corrupting memories⌐⌐ of childhood, . . .

Cloture refers to a full stop at the end of a line, couplet, or other stanzaic unit:

"I love your hair that way," she said⌐⌐

Semi-cloture takes place when the end of the line coincides with the end of a phrase or clause:

> Mutually grappled, we ate the fruit `[==]`
>   its skin and core—and quaffed flesh deeply `[:]`
> dampening our solitude `[;]` . . .

Enjambment is the opposite of cloture: lines run on. *Grammatic enjambment* is the running on of a sentence, without pause, from one line or stanza to the next:

> the tragicomic masks of age⌐
>
> ⌐and youth must come at last to tatters.

Metrical enjambment takes place when, in effect, half the verse foot belonging to a following line occurs at the end of the preceding line:

> ˘ ´ | ˘ ´ | ˘ ˘ ´
> its skin and core—and quaffed flesh deeply,
>
> ´ | ˘ : | ˘ ˘ ´ | ˘˘
> dampening our solitude, . . .

It can perhaps be seen more easily like this:

> ˘ ´ | ˘ ´ | ˘ ˘ ´ ˘ , / ´ | ˘ : | ˘
> its skin and core—and quaffed flesh deeply, / dampening our
>
> ´ | ˘˘
> solitude, . . .

The reverse can also take place—half the verse foot belonging to a preceding line is added to the beginning of the following line. Here is the complete poem:

Party Game

> "I love your hair that way," she said.
>   We sought through rooms for something warm
> enough. We tested miles of bed,
> Lay on an open moor that spread
>   beyond fourposters and the dawn.
>
> Mutually grappled, we ate the fruit—
>   its skin and core—and quaffed flesh deeply,
> dampening our solitude,

corrupting memories of childhood,
   slipping into age too steeply.

"It's not the way I thought it was,"
   she said. So I was Adam damned
again for female niches and flaws.
Thus, we deserted mattress moors,
   returned, wise now, to parlor games.

And spin the bottle all our days—
   no game's a turn that really matters.
Though minds have likened worlds to stages,
the tragicomic masks of age,
   and of youth, must come at last to tatters.

                        —L.T.

Elision is the blending of two or more syllable sounds so that they become one syllable sound. There are various ways of eliding:

1. *Vocalic elision*—Robert Bridges in his book *Milton's Prosody* (Oxford, 1893) describes vocalic elision. "When two vowel sounds come together, then if the first of the two has a tail-glide (a *y*-glide or a *w*-glide), there may be elision." Some examples of y-glide are fl*y*ing, so b*e* *i*t, th*e* *o*thers, th*ee* *a*nd sh*e* *a*nd all, glor*y* *a*bove, and r*i*ot. Some examples of w-glide are r*u*inous, s*o* *o*ften, als*o* *i*n, Morocc*o* *o*r Trebisond, fol*lowers* (foll'wers), sha*dowy* (shad'wy), grad-*ual*, infl*ue*nce.

2. *Semi-vocalic elision*—Bridges suggests in his book that, "If two unstressed vowels be separated by *r*, there may be elision." Donald Justice, in his samizdat notes *Of Prosody* (Iowa City, 1960), adds, "This applies also to *l* and *n* and perhaps may be extended to *m*." Some examples are mur*mur*ing (murm'ring), pill*ar of* state (pillar 'f state), car*ol*er (car'ler), and begott*en a*nd (begot'n and).

3. *Overt elision*—In certain kinds of obsolete poetic diction, overt elision (as in the parenthetical examples just above) occurs where the writer indicates what has been elided by means of punctuation. Other kinds of overt elision are in everyday use, as in don't, can't, would've, and so forth.

4. *Consonantal silence*—Bridges says, "H is often considered as no letter," as in ought t*o* *ha*ve (ought to 'ave or ought to've, where

the following vowel is also suppressed: I've, you've—see vocalic suppression below). Other consonants are sometimes silent as well, as in *often* (of'en or of'n).

5. *Consonantal suppression*—Justice says, "Final *m* and *n* are very frequently not counted anyhow, as *chasm* or *heaven* [heav'n]." *Vocalic suppression.* Justice continues, "The words *evil* [ev'l] and *spirit* [spir't] have also been taken in English verse to have but one syllable." Vocalic suppression sometimes takes place after a silent consonant as well, as in *ought to've* and *of'n*.

6. *Counter-elision*—"In contrast," Justice says, "*fire* [fi-er] often is counted as two [syllables in length]." The same is true for other words—*hire, mire, lyre*—and in many dialects words are pronounced as though they had more syllables than usual—*repair* (re-pay-er; see section on dialect rhyme that follows).

7. *Option*—"Elision in most of these words," Justice says, "is optional; that is, the word need not be elided each time it occurs, even if it occurs twice in the same line." The same is true of counter-elision.

When we were considering the Robert Burns stanza, we noted that the lines were of different lengths:

A Red, Red Rose

O, my luve's like a red, red rose,
    That's newly sprung in June:
O, my luve's like the melodie
    That's sweetly played in tune.

As fair art thou, my bonie lass,
    So deep in luve am I:
And I will luve thee still, my dear,
    Till a' the seas gang dry.

Till a' the seas gang dry, my dear,
    And the rocks melt wi' the sun:
I will luve thee still, my dear,
    While the sands o'life shall run.

And fare thee weel, my only luve,
    And fare thee weel awhile!

And I will come again, my luve,
   Tho' it were ten thousand mile.
          —ROBERT BURNS

You might suppose that these differing line-lengths indicate that this poem is quantitative verse, by analogy with quantitative syllabics and quantitative accentuals, *but this assumption would not be correct.* This poem is *normative* accentual-syllabics because there is a running foot: all the lines are iambic, only their lengths differ. The first and third lines of each stanza are tetrameter, the second and fourth are trimeter, and that is how the poem must be described.

The prosody of the classical Greeks depended upon a system in which each syllable was assigned its particular length or *duration,* much as notes in a musical scale can be eighth notes, quarter notes, half notes, or whole notes. Some English poets, particularly in the Renaissance, experimented with quantitative accentual-syllabics, assigning to English syllables specific lengths. None of these experiments was successful. English intonations remained basically strong-stress, and no quantitative codification of stress, duration, pitch, or intonation ever took place.

The one thing that did take hold in English poetics, however, was the nomenclature of the Greek verse feet—these names were applied (in fact, *mis*applied) to English stress prosody when accentual-syllabic prosody was being rediscovered in the sixteenth century.

As we have seen, the ancient English prosody, introduced by the Anglo-Saxons from Scandinavia, was strong-stress accentual verse. Before the Angles, Saxons, and Jutes, the literary language of England was classical Latin, which had been introduced by the occupying Romans and reintroduced by the Roman Catholic Church. Latin verse imitated classical Greek prosody, but the native singers of England knew nothing of it. The medieval prosody of the Celtic outlands of Great Britain was syllabic, as we have mentioned. Accentual prosody and syllabic prosody lived side-by-side for centuries in Britain without influencing one another.

In 1066, however, the Norman French invaded England and brought with them the French syllabic prosody. The Normans were the same race as the Anglo-Saxons—both were "Northmen"—but the former had been acculturated to French civilization. For several centuries, then, until about 1300 or so, the official literary language of Great Britain was French. The conquerors wrote poetry in French syllabics, while the Englishmen continued to write in alliterative accentuals.

Gradually, the two languages merged. The Germanic Old English lost many of its endings and inflections and adopted many French words. The result was that Old English and French became Middle English. Enter Geoffrey Chaucer, John Gower, and some others who were confronted with a problem. The prosodic tradition in which they had been educated was Norman French, and the French do not believe there are accents, except occasionally, in their tongue; therefore, they are prevented from accounting for stresses and must count only syllables, if they are to count anything. (If the French count nothing, they believe they write *vers libre* or "free verse," a term that, when it was accepted into American poetic terminology early in this century, caused as much confusion about what constituted prose and verse as it has done in France.)

The English Chaucerians, however, could *hear* the stresses of Middle English, and they felt they could not ignore the English half of their heritage. They therefore invented accentual-syllabic prosody, counting all syllables, stressed syllables, and, in effect, verse feet, though they had no names for such things.

With the death of Chaucer and Gower about 1400, poets generally forgot about accentual-syllabics. The Scots, however, kept the tradition (and the Middle English language) alive, though the bards of the Scottish borders slipped halfway back to strong-stress verse and wrote their folk ballads in podic prosody.

A century later (about 1500), John Skelton was writing in both podics and accentual-syllabics. Some critics consider Skelton to be the last English Medieval poet, others think of him as the first Renaissance poet. He was both. His successors rediscovered Chaucer's prosody, looked around for names to apply to the measures they discovered, and used the Greek terms that were at hand during that age of discovery and rediscovery.

They also began writing an approximation of classical quantitative prosody. They *preassigned* kinds and numbers of verse feet in a line *in a particular order*. SAPPHICS will serve as an example. A Sapphic line contains two trochees, followed by a dactyl, followed by two trochees. In a Sapphic stanza, which is a quatrain, there are three such lines followed by an ADONIC line, which is a dactyl followed by a trochee. Here is one Sapphic line followed by one adonic:

Visitor, you've come and have gone while I was . . .

darkling with questions.

For this whole poem, see "Visitor" in my *Poetry: An Introduction Through Writing* (Reston, Va., 1973). For other sapphic poems (and examples of many of the forms to be found here), see *Strong Measures,* edited by Philip Dacey and David Jauss (New York, 1986). I shall have many occasions to refer to these books, and to Alberta Turner's *Poets Teaching* (New York, 1980), in the ensuing pages.

Variable accentual-syllabics mixes line-lengths, although there is a running foot. An example is the first strophe of William Wordsworth's "Ode: Intimations of Immortality from Recollections of Early Childhood." The small letters to the right of the poem indicate the rhymes; the superscript numbers indicate the line-lengths:

There was a time when meadow, grove, and stream, a^5

The earth and every common sight, b^4

To me did seem a^2

Appareled in celestial light, b^4

The glory and the freshness of a dream. a^5

It is not now as it hath been of yore— c^5

Turn whereso'er I may, d^3

By night or day, d^2

The things which I have seen I now can see no

more. c^6

In this poem, the normative meter is constant (with some variations), but the line-lengths and rhyming pattern are random.

The *general form* of this poem is the ODE, as indicated by its title. An ode is a solemn poem written to celebrate an occasion. Although there are set forms for the ode, this particular example does not follow either a poem-form or a stanza-form; it therefore has no *specific form*.

As we have noted, the *Celtic forms* are syllabic; however, certain of them specify that stressed syllables appear in certain places. For instance, in the Irish DEIBHIDHE, a quatrain stanza, it is a requirement that the last syllable in line one (1) and line three (3) be stressed. Thus, though the main metric is syllabic, there is also an accentual component. Such verse must logically be called *syllabic-accentuals*.

INVENTED PROSODIES

The English language has borrowed and absorbed so much from other languages and cultures that there are limitless possibilities for invention within it. For instance, it is possible to postulate a prosody based upon *counting only unstressed syllables in a line of verse,* paying no attention to the stressed syllables, of which there might be any number. Although this *moraic* prosody would look and read like prose, it would in fact be a verse prosody.

PROPORTION IN RHYME

There are various kinds of rhyme and other devices for making words *chime* against one another. Some have already been discussed, including *alliteration* and *cynghanedd. True rhyme* has to do with the identical sound, in two or more words, of an accented vowel (ó - ó - ó) as well as of all the sounds following that vowel (one - óan - ówn), while the consonantal sounds immediately preceding the vowel differ in each word (bóne - lóan - shówn).

End rhyme rhymes line endings:

> One science only will one genius fit;
> So vast is art, so narrow human wit.
> **—ALEXANDER POPE** from *Essay on Criticism*

Falling rhyme (feminine rhyme) means a rhyming of lines of verse with falling meters or feminine endings:

fálling - cálling.

Falling rhythms begin with an accented syllable and end with an unaccented syllable. Dactyls and trochees are falling meters. *Rising rhyme* (masculine rhyme) is a rhyming of lines of verse with rising meters or masculine endings:

aríse - despíse.

Rising rhythms begin with an unaccented syllable and end with an accented syllable. Anapests and iambs are rising meters. *Light rhyme* rhymes a falling ending with a rising ending:

fálling - ríng.

Internal rhyme rhymes the ending of a line with a word in the center of the same line, usually with a syllable just before the caesura, as in the third line of the following quatrain from "The Man in the Man-Made Moon":

Coal black is the raven, coal black is the rook,
Coal black is the shark in the billow.
Where I once had a *Bill* · to drive back my *chill*
There's a cold blackeyed pea on my pillow.
                                        —X. J. KENNEDY

Linked rhyme rhymes the last syllable or syllables of a line with the first syllable or syllables of the following line (The bell is heard, and the song is *sung* / *Flung* upon the morning air). *Interlaced rhyme* rhymes a syllable or syllables in the center of a line with a syllable or syllables in the center of the preceding or following line (The song is *sung*, and the bell is heard / It is *flung* upon the air). *Cross rhyme* rhymes an ending with a sound at the center of the preceding or following line (The bell is heard, and the song is *sung*; / The sound is *flung* on the morning air).

Head rhyme rhymes syllables at the beginnings of lines of verse (*Sung* is the song of the ringing bell / *flung* upon the morning air). *Apocopated rhyme* drops one or more syllables from the ending of one of a pair of rhyming words (The bells were ringing on the *morn-* / ing that the song of the sun was *born*). *Enjambed rhyme* uses the first consonant of the following line to complete the sound of the rhyme (He found the stair, and *he* / *d*escended to find the *seed*).

Single rhymes are rhymes of one syllable (morn - born); *double rhymes*, of two syllables (singing - ringing), and *triple rhymes* of three syllables (intending - descending). *Compound rhyme* treats groups of words as though they were one-word rhymes, as in the poem "Song—Ruth" from W. S. Gilbert's *The Pirates of Penzance*:

A nurserymaid is not afraid of what you people *call* work,
So I made up my mind to go as a kind of piratical maid-of-all-
work.

Mosaic rhyme uses one compound ending and one normal
ending in a rhyme, illustrated here from the same song and
source:

And that is how you find me now, a member of your shy lot,
Which you wouldn't have found, had he been bound apprentice
to a pilot.

Trite rhyme is the rhyming of words that have been overused
for rhymes. Joyce Kilmer's "Trees" is an easily found model
of many of the trite rhymes in the English language. Popular
songs are another source of reference. It is possible for trite
rhymes to be used in original and interesting ways, however,
for much of their triteness has to do with their contex-
tual use.

Omoioteleton is a classical term that covers the various
types of rhyme other than true rhyme. *Rich rhyme* (*rime
riche,* false rhyme) has identical sound in the consonants im-
mediately preceding the accented vowel as well as in the
sounds following it (c´yst, pers´ist, ins´ist). It is really a form
of repetition rather than rhyme. *Consonance* (meaning "like-
sounds"—not to be confused with *consonants*) has also been
called *slant rhyme, off-rhyme,* and *near-rhyme.* It substitutes
s´imilar sound for identical sound (bri´dge, he´dge, go´uge,
ra´ge, ro´uge). Consonance assumes that all vowel sounds are
interchangeable with one another, as are certain related con-
sonant sounds such as the soft *g* in "gouge" and "rage," the
harder *dg* of "bridge" and "hedge," and the *zh* sound of
"rouge." The verb form of the noun is "to consonate."

Analyzed rhyme is a system Edward Davison described in
his book *Some Modern Poets* (New York, 1928): "[He] takes
two such words as *soon* and *hide* but separates the vowel from
the consonantal sounds before looking for his rhymes. The

oo of *soon* is united with the *d* of *hide;* and the *i* of *hide* with
the *n* of *soon.* This simple analysis produces the [four] rhym-
ing sounds

oon   ine
ide   ood

as a basis for new sets of words. Thus, by means of analyzed
rhyme, an absolute sound relationship can be established
among words that have hitherto seemed alien to each other."
Words that might use the sounds presented above would be
moon, divine, chide, and *brood.* See "Winter" in the entry on
the QUATRAIN for an example of a poem that uses analyzed
rhyme.

Wrenched rhyme is as much pun as anything else. It twists
words to make rhymes, as Ogden Nash did in his prose
poem titled "Kindly Unhitch That Star, Buddy": "Some
people think they will eventually wear diamonds instead of
rhinestones / Only by everlastingly keeping their noses to
their ghrinestones, . . ." *Amphisbaenic rhyme* is "backward"
rhyme; that is, words are either spelled backward (see *ortho-
graphical schemas* in chapter 5) or pronounced backward
(later - retail, stop - pots, Potsdam - madstop, pets - instep).
Lyon rime, described by George Puttenham in his *The Arte of
English Poesie* (1589; reprint edition, Kent, Ohio, 1970) is
really not rhyme at all, though it is a form of repetition. It is,
in fact, a *constructional schema* (see chapter 5). Some verses are
written that, when read backward word for word beginning
with the last word, say exactly the opposite of what the
verses originally said, as in this quatrain by Wesli Court:

"One in heat can love cool"—
Believe, and remain her fool.
Fool her. Remain, and believe
Cool love can heat in one.

Sight Rhyme (*eye-rhyme*) is orthographic rhyming; sight-
rhymed words are spelled alike but they sound different

(*eight - sleight, ties -* homi*lies*). *Dialect rhyme* is often difficult to distinguish from sight rhyme. People from different places, or from different eras ("historical rhyme"), might pronounce the same word differently; that is, one person will pronounce "again" so that it rhymes with "pain," but another person will rhyme it with "pen."

Echo has to do with the reappearance of identical sounds or with the appearance of similar sounds. For instance, *parimion,* the classical term for *alliteration* (which has already been discussed) is the repetition of stressed *initial* consonant sounds in a series of words. Note that the stressed sound must be *the first syllable* in the word, not a second or later syllable (He *t*ucked in his *t*unic and *t*ore it *t*erribly). *Assonance* repeats identically stressed vowel sounds anywhere in a word (The c*á*t was indef*á*tigable in its att*á*ck on the r*á*t). *Consonantal echo* has to do with the repetition of consonants, both stressed and unstressed, whether at the beginnings of words or elsewhere, and not necessarily in sequence:

If she were al*i*ve he'd *l*o*v*e her sti*ll*.

Vocalic echo is the repetition of vowels, both stressed and unstressed, whether at the beginnings of words or elsewhere:

If sh*e* were al*i*ve h*e*'d l*i*ke her st*i*ll.

Cynghanedd, a system incorporating rhyme, alliteration, assonance, and vocalic and consonantal echo, has been discussed earlier in these pages.

Onomatopoeia "describes" something through sound, the sonics of the passage imitating the subject (The seashore roared from the seashell's horn). *Euphony* is a mingling of pleasant sounds, usually including all vowels and certain consonants: soft c, f, soft g, h, j, l, m, n, r, s, v, w, y, and z. *Dissonance* is a mingling of unpleasant sounds, usually hard consonants. *Cacophony* is an unpleasant mixture of sounds both euphonious and dissonant.

Repetition refers to the reappearance of sounds, words, phrases, and lines. A *repeton* is a single line or phrase repeated *once* after its initial appearance in a poem. A *repetend* is a single line or phrase that reappears more than once after its initial appearance, but at random. A *refrain* is a single phrase or line that reappears at formal intervals throughout a poem, usually at the end of each stanza. A *burden* is similar to a refrain, except that it consists of a couplet or something larger. A *chorus* is a whole stanza that appears at intervals during the progress of the poem. *Incremental repetition* is a repeton, repetend, refrain, burden, or chorus with at least one word changed each time it reappears, so that the line takes on greater significance as the poem moves toward a climax. Folk ballads, such as "Lord Randal," and nursery rhymes, such as "Robbin to Bobbin," illustrate various techniques of repetition. For discussions of these two poems, see my *Poetry: An Introduction* (op. cit.).

Proportion has to do with various kinds of balance in a poem. *Proportion by situation of rhyme* has to do with the arrangement of rhymes in a stanza by distance. First distance is *couplet rhyme* (*aa*); second distance is *triplet rhyme* (*aba*); third distance is *envelope stanza quatrain* (*abba*); fourth distance is *quintet envelope,* where the rhyme leaps three lines of *b* rhyme (*abbba*) or a triplet rhyme (*abcba*).

Proportion by situation of measures is concerned with variations in lengths of lines in a stanza; that is, the patterns of long and short lines. An example is found in the stanza called STANDARD HABBIE, where the lines are sometimes of four feet, sometimes of two feet (the numerals here indicate length-of-line): $a^4a^4a^4b^2a^4b^2$.

Proportion in figure has to do with the typographical level—choosing the appropriate stanza shape to suit the poem. Often lines of the same length will be indented or will start at the margin. Similarly, the poet might or might not indent, according to the rhyme scheme. Capitalizing the initial letters of lines is also an option. *Proportion by treatment* means choosing the appropriate meters, forms, and lengths (both

of lines and of the whole poem) to deal with the subject and
theme of the poem.

NOTATION

Notation deals with the shorthand recordings of the rhyme
schemes and line-lengths in poems. The first rhyme sound
of a poem is always noted as *a,* and whenever that rhyme
sound reappears, it is again recorded as *a.* The second rhyme
is *b,* the third, *c,* and so on. The numerals above the small
letters (a^4) indicate length-of-line (in this case, four verse
feet).

When a line is used as a refrain, the first refrain will, if it is
also the first rhyme, be noted with a capital letter *A,* the sec-
ond refrain, if the second rhyme, will be capital *B,* and so
forth. If there are two refrains in the poem with the *same
rhyme,* they are differentiated by numerals: A^1bA^2, as in the
VILLANELLE, for instance. If you wish to indicate line-lengths
as well, a second numeral will indicate line-length, the first
indicating the refrain (see the PANTOUM, which is built en-
tirely of repeated lines).

A particular system of metrical notation was developed
for, and copyrighted in, *The Book of Forms* (New York,
1968), and it is retained here. The schematic diagrams that
appear beneath most of the prose descriptions of the various
poetic forms, lines, and stanza patterns in Part II are de-
signed to present visually (1) the number of syllables in each
line of verse; (2) the number of accents in each line; (3) the
rhyme schemes; and (4) the positions of rhymed and un-
rhymed refrains and repetitions. For these reasons, the tradi-
tional method of scansion is not used, and the following
symbols should be noted:

x   —Small x stands for an unrhymed syllable that
is either unaccented or whose accent is
unimportant. Please note that *the breve symbol
is not necessary under these circumstances, and it is
not used.*

	—An accent mark stands for an accent (stress).
x	—Stands for an unrhymed, *accented* syllable.
a, b, c . . .	—Small letters other than x stand for rhymes.
á, b́, ć . . .	—Small accented letters other than x stand for stressed rhymed syllables.
A, B, C . . .	—1. In the Welsh and Irish forms, capital letters stand for *main* rhymes. —2. In the French forms, capital letters (except R) indicate *rhymed refrains that are whole lines or repetons.*
R	—In some French forms, R indicates a *refrain that consists of only a part of a line.*
A¹, B¹, A², B²	—Numbered capital letters indicate *sequence of refrains;* see the example of the PANTOUM.
or	—In certain Welsh forms, "or" indicates a syllable or word that *consonates* (off-rhyming or slant-rhyming).
oe, ay, ei . . .	—In certain Welsh forms, grouped letters (other than *ex*es and *or*) indicate *dipththong rhymes.*
c, xc, bc . . .	—In certain Irish forms, a small c used alone or grouped with other letters indicates *consonance,* not rhyme.
*x*x, x*a*x, xxx*b*	—Otherwise, grouped letters indicate a *word* consisting of that many syllables.
x x *a* x x	—In the Welsh and Irish forms, *italicized* syllables indicate *possible positions* for rhymes, cross-rhymes, assonances, or alliterations.

Although these symbols might seem confusing out of context, they will become immediately clear when you consult the schematic diagrams themselves. There will be certain exceptions to these notation rules, but in each case the exceptions will be apparent and will be stated in the heading for each form.

4 The Sensory Level

A *trope* is a "figure of speech": certain language constructions present figures to the eye, to the ear, to the other senses, and these representations appeal to the inner "sense" of emotion. A trope makes a mind-picture; it is descriptive in nature.

DESCRIPTIVE TROPES

Descriptions are simple tropes, but not all tropes are descriptions. In fact, the most effective figures of speech are more complex than adjectives and adjective phrases modifying nouns (pretty girl, kettle of fish), or adverbs and adverbial constructions modifying adjectives (very pretty), verbs (run fast) or other adverbs (jump really high). Heightened language uses few modifiers but many tropes of a more sophisticated and effective kind.

Hypotiposis is the description of real things; *pragmatographia* is the description of actions; *topographia* is description of real places; *chronographia* is description of seasons, times of day, and so forth. *Icon* is word portraiture. *Prosopographia* is description of a person one has never known—imaginative portraiture. *Enigma* is a deliberately obscure description, as in a riddle.

A *neologism* is a coined word, one invented by a particular writer. An *epithetic compound* is two descriptive words made into one—"deathgush," "thickdark," "sunbright," and so forth. One form of the epithetic compound is the *portmanteau word* of Lewis Carroll, which combines parts of two different words; for instance, "slithy" is made out of *lithe* and *slimy*. Carroll intended the overtones or *associations* the reader has with both words to continue being present in the new word. A *kenning* is a brief metaphorical synonym; for instance, "the whale's road" equals the ocean. Kennings are a prominent feature of Anglo-Saxon stress verse poetry. An *oxymoron* is a descriptive phrase that combines terms that seem mutually exclusive but, in context, are not—"sweet bitterness," "terrible beauty," "burning chill," and so forth.

SIMILETIC TROPES

Omiosis is examination by similarity: two things in some way resemble each other. *Comparisons* examine similar things: Her smile was *like* the sun, *as* warm *as* morning light upon the rose.

Analogy is the means by which simile proceeds: comparing things that are not identical (He stood as if he were an oak braced against the wind). In this example, "He" is the subject of the simile, and "oak" is the *analogue,* the trope that bears the weight of the comparison.

Contrast examines different things: (The lake was no more a mirror than the sky is a pancake).

Allusion is comparison by reference to something outside the poem, or to something not organically a part of the poem (He came, *like Rome,* to see, and stayed to conquer).

Parabola is resemblance by imagery, talking about one thing in terms of something entirely different in kind. Yeats used parabola in "Crazy Jane and the Bishop" when Crazy Jane says, "But a birch-tree stood my Jack: / *The solid man and the coxcomb.*"

METAPHORICAL TROPES

The nature of *allegory* is to speak about one subject in terms of another, allowing the subject to become new again, making it clearer and sharper. The heart of allegory is *metaphor*. An allegory is a story told on two levels simultaneously. First there is the *narrative* level on which, for instance, we have a story about an ugly duckling. Corresponding to the narrative level *at every point* is the *symbolic level*—what we are *really* talking about—in this case, an ugly child without a doubt. The moral is, "You will grow up to be a beautiful adult, just like the ugly duckling who turned into a swan." There is even an *implied* extension of the moral in this story: "You will outstrip the ordinary people who laugh at you now."

No matter how much a substantive or verb is qualified by means of modifiers, it remains essentially unchanged. Metaphor changes a word essentially by making it equivalent to something else, something different: "The sun and moon are coins to be spent lightly or in dark ways." In this example, the language equation is *sun + moon = coins*. A metaphor that is extended beyond the original equation is called a *conceit* (an obsolete spelling for the word "concept"). In our example, the conceit following the equation consists of *to be spent* (like money, like time), *lightly* (a pun, meaning "in a carefree way" or "without much thought," at the same time continuing the metaphor of sun *light* or day *light*), and *in dark ways* (in ways that are hopeless or despairing, perhaps also evoking nighttime).

The *tenor* is the subject of a metaphor; it is the thing being talked about. The object of a metaphor is called the *vehicle;* it is the *trope* that bears the weight of the equation between the two things or qualities that, nevertheless, have a point or points in common. *Sun and moon* are the compound tenor of our example; *coins* is the vehicle. Roundness is the perceived point in common between *coins* and *sun and moon*. Extended points in common, implied by the *context* of our equation, are that the day's coin, the sun, is golden, and that the night's coin, the moon, is silver.

Sometimes the subject about which we wish to speak is an abstract concept, for there are two kinds of nouns in language. An *abstract noun* is any substantive open to broad and various definition (e.g., "soul," "truth," "beauty," "justice,"

"God," "love"). A *concrete noun* is any substantive that can be conventionally defined (e.g., table, brick, rug, tree, elephant, house). An *anchored abstraction* is an abstract noun metaphorized by being equated with a concrete noun that, thus, defines it: "Her heart is a stone." *Denotation* is the primary meaning or *dictionary definition* of a word: "*Heart. A bodily organ, the purpose of which is to circulate the blood.*" *Connotation* is an ancillary or secondary meaning of a word. Connotations of *heart* are courage, as in "He has great heart"; love, as in "An affair of the heart"; and essence, as in "He is pure of heart."

Context is the environment in which a word is situated in a phrase, clause, or larger grammatical unit. This environment limits the denotations and connotations of the word. In "Her heart is a stone," we understand that she is *hard-hearted,* an idiomatic expression meaning *without pity.* In "His heart beat strongly in battle," the context of the word heart allows the denotation *a bodily organ* and the connotation *courage,* but it eliminates the other connotations of *love* and *essence.*

Overtone is this allowance of connotations by context. In "The sun and moon are coins to be spent lightly, or in dark ways," context allows the denotation of carefreeness in "lightly," as well as the connotation of "brightness"—and thereby "gold"—through overtone created by a *subdued metaphor* (metaphor implied, not stated, by the context). Overtone amplifies meaning, thereby making it *ambiguous* and *inclusive* but not obscure.

Obscurity blocks meanings, as when a poet refers to one abstraction in terms of another—an *unanchored abstraction.* Keats' "'Beauty is truth, truth beauty,'—that is all / Ye know on earth, and all ye need to know," the last two lines of his "Ode on a Grecian Urn," is an unanchored abstraction. It means nothing, or, rather, it means anything the reader wishes it to mean. It is not a metaphor because there is no discernible point in common between the two abstractions, and there is no way to tell which abstract noun is the tenor and which the vehicle. Fortunately, the rest of the poem provides a context for these lines that gives the reader a feeling for what the poet might have been talking about, at least as far as "beauty" is concerned if not for "truth."

A poem can be *exclusive* or *inclusive*. The poet can build contexts that limit meanings severely or, instead, that amplify the poem through overtone and symbology. A *symbol* is a concretion that represents an abstraction, for example, in some contexts, the ocean is symbolic of eternity. An *emblem* is a conventional symbol (a bald eagle is emblematic of the United States of America). William Empson, in his book *Seven Types of Ambiguity* (New York, 1955), listed ambiguities that can add to the inclusive quality of a poem:

First type ambiguities arise when a detail is effective in several ways at once, e.g., by comparisons with several points of likeness, antitheses with several points of difference, "comparative" adjectives, subdued metaphors, and extra meanings suggested by rhythm.

Second type ambiguities arise when two or more alternative meanings are fully resolved into one.

Third type ambiguities arise when two apparently unconnected meanings are given simultaneously.

Fourth type ambiguities arise when the alternative meanings combine to make clear a complicated state of mind in the author.

Fifth type ambiguities arise when [there is] a fortunate confusion, as when the author is discovering his idea in the act of writing . . . or not holding it all at once.

Sixth type ambiguities arise when what is said is contradictory or irrelevant and the reader is forced to invent interpretations. [This, in fact, is obscurity, not ambiguity.]

Seventh type ambiguities [occur when there is] full contradiction, marking a division in the author's mind.

For more discussion of overtone, see the entry on the HAIKU.

Besides those metaphoric constructions already named, there are (1) *synesthesia,* talking about one of the senses in terms of another: "The afternoon smelled blue" (scent-sight), "I could taste her sweet whispers" (taste-hearing), "He touched me with his mind" (touch-thought); (2) *dimin-*

ishing metaphor, which has a deliberately overintense or overstated tenor in relation to its vehicle: "*The burning moon* that she remembers / Was but a brand of dying *embers*"; (3) *organic metaphor,* which rises logically from the context; (4) *gratuitous metaphor,* which does not logically arise from the context; and (5) *dyfalu,* a Welsh term that describes a tenor that bursts into a profusion of vehicles (in other words, a catalog vehicle): "The *moon* was a *coin,* a *ring* of fire, / A *cartwheel* rolling across the sky, / A *heaven* full of lightning turning / Around the earth, a cosmic *pyre.*" Additionally, *paradox* is an antithetical metaphor or statement that combines terms that seem mutually exclusive (see the aforementioned *oxymoron*) but, in fact, are not: "*Freedom* is the *prison of rebellion,*" or "*Winter* is the *spring of contemplation.*" Paradox can also be a statement that contradicts a commonly held belief: "The earth is not round, it is egg-shaped."

The final metaphoric construction is called *prosopopeia.* Prosopopeia is *personification,* speaking of nonhuman things in human terms, as Keats does in his "Ode to Autumn," where fall is referred to as the "Close bosom-friend of the maturing sun." The *pathetic fallacy* is absurd or overstated personification—endowing nonhuman things with bathetic or pathetic qualities, often through *cue words* (such as *apple pie, motherhood, love, truth, beauty, teddy bear,* etc.) that our culture has conditioned us to respond to automatically. Such words are meant to induce unthinking sentimental responses in the reader. In the phrase, "The little white cloud that cried," *little, cloud,* and *cried* are cues. Similarly, in Joyce Kilmer's "Trees" the undiscriminating reader will simultaneously see the tree as a mother figure, an infant figure, and a religious figure. Some thought, however, will bring all the images together logically and come up with the image of a monster with hair for leaves, eyes on stalks tangled in the hair, a mouth at the bottom of an elongated head buried in the earth, and so forth. If too much emotional weight is placed upon the nonhuman vehicle of a metaphor, the pathetic fallacy is likely to occur. To say, "I cried like a little white cloud" is one thing, but to lose sight of the tenor "I" and say, "The little white cloud cried" is another: inanimate objects cannot cry.

The term *catachresis* implies the misuse of tropes. Every poem must make "sense"—not necessarily *logical* sense, but *poetic* sense in context. If a metaphor or other trope simply makes no "sense" of any kind—for instance, where the context does not block out enough connotations, causing confusion about what a word means (at which point, ambiguity becomes obscurity)—then the trope is catachretic. A *mixed metaphor* is catachretic because its vehicle is inappropriate to the tenor (The sun and moon are baby buggies) or because the vehicle itself is made up of inappropriate elements (Keep your nose to the grindstone, your shoulder to the wheel, and an eye peeled for trouble).

TRADITIONAL USES OF TROPES

There are various *traditions* for using descriptions, similes, and metaphors. Symbolism uses *archetypes,* or those universal symbols for the great basic drives and abstract concepts of human existence. An archetype is the original thing from which a copy is made. Some psychoanalysts, including Carl Jung, believe that certain myths are genetically transmitted from generation to generation through the "collective unconscious," or race memory. To use the archetypal symbol, the poet must find the key to those memories, not through logic, but through what T. S. Eliot called the *objective correlative*—the object or word that, in and of itself, produces the *image of the idea* in the reader. The idea is not stated; rather, the poet proceeds by intuition, choosing words that, like incantations or charms, conjure up from the blood those feelings, mysteries, and terrors that have been represented through various symbols since man became man. Although

the symbols vary from epoch to epoch, they remain the same
at their core, they remain the archetypes, the ancient proto-
types of elemental mystery:

The Tyger

Tyger! Tyger! burning bright
In the forests of the night,
What immortal hand or eye
Could frame thy fearful symmetry?

In what distant deeps or skies
Burnt the fire of thine eyes?
On what wings dare he aspire?
What the hand dare seize the fire?

And what shoulder, & what art,
Could twist the sinews of thy heart?
And when thy heart began to beat,
What dread hand? & what dread feet?

What the hammer? what the chain?
In what furnace was thy brain?
What the anvil? what dread grasp
Dare its deadly terrors clasp?

When the stars threw down their spears,
And water'd heaven with their tears,
Did he smile his work to see?
Did he who made the Lamb make thee?

Tyger! Tyger! burning bright
In the forests of the night,
What immortal hand or eye
Could frame thy fearful symmetry?

—WILLIAM BLAKE

Impressionism uses images to create moods; *surrealism* dis-
torts reality. William Carlos Williams coined *imagism*'s slo-
gan, "No ideas but in things"—that is, if the appropriate ve-
hicle is chosen, there is no need to mention the tenor, the
subject, or the theme, which will rise organically out of the

vehicle. *Metaphysical* poetry is really *metaphorical* poetry, and it proceeds by using the extended metaphor, the *conceit:*

The Sun Rising

Busy old fool, unruly Sun,
Why dost thou thus,
Through windows, and through curtains, call on us?
Must to thy motions lovers' seasons run?
Saucy pedantic wretch, go chide
Late school-boys and sour prentices,
Go tell court-huntsmen that the king will ride,
Call country ants to harvest offices;
Love, all alike, no season knows nor clime,
Nor hours, days, months, which are the rags of time.

Thy beams so reverend and strong
Why shouldst thou think?
I could eclipse and cloud them with a wink,
But that I would not lose her sight so long.
If her eyes have not blinded thine,
Look, and tomorrow late tell me,
Whether both th' Indias of spice and mine
Be where thou left'st them, or lie here with me.
Ask for those kings whom thou saw'st yesterday,
And thou shalt hear, "All here in one bed lay."

She's all states, and all princes I;
Nothing else is.
Princes do but play us; compared to this,
All honor's mimic, all wealth alchemy.
Thou, Sun, art half as happy as we,
In that the world's contracted thus;
Thine age asks ease, and since thy duties be
To warm the world, that's done in warming us.
Shine here to us, and thou art everywhere;
This bed thy centre is, these walls thy sphere.

—JOHN DONNE

RHETORICAL TROPES

Rhetoric is the art of effective speaking and writing; it creates an effect in the listener and affects him as well. Some tropes are called rhetorical tropes because they create their effects through nonmetaphorical figures of speech. In the examples given below, an asterisk (*) marks those passages taken from Wesli Court's dipodic satire of contemporary poetry, *Odds Bodkin's Strange Thrusts and Ravels,* found in my *Poetry: An Introduction* (op. cit.).

Anachinosis refers the reader, in an argument, to his own opinion:

> Odds wishes you godspeed,
> sirs. Go out and read
> if you believe not
> this rave and riot.
> Pick up a book, buy it,
> peruse it—then, once you have done,
> use it as best it suits you.*

Antenagoge makes a statement, then softens it by adding a mitigating or less harsh alternative (I wish, my dear, that you'd fall over dead— / Well, maybe just fall down and hit your head).

Antiphrasis is derision by means of simple contradiction; for example, calling a fat man "skinny" or a thin man "fatso."

Antipophora is asking a question, then answering it oneself, for instance, when a scarecrow asks a field full of pumpkins, "You worship me? a pole for a spine, a / timber for my extended bone, fingers / of hay stolen by wrens?" he answers himself, "I bleach and shake, / I shudder in the moon's dark. Pumpkins, crowd of orange globes, I whistle in the wind."

Antitheton is the term for the technique of becoming "the devil's advocate" in argument: taking any position and defending it simply for the joy of a fight, or to bring out some point that might otherwise remain unexamined.

Aporia expresses doubt or uncertainty.

Apostrophe is direct address—speaking to an absent human being or to a (usually) personified thing or abstraction, as Keats does in the "Ode to Autumn."

Asteismus is simple jesting, without rancor (Did Samson Ago-nistes have the strength / Of twenty bulls at cowtime in the spring?).

Charientismus is light banter meant to soothe rancor.

Dialisis sets up the propositions of an argument. These proposi-tions are a dilemma in that they seem mutually exclusive: it must be one or the other proposition, but which? Perhaps it is neither, or both: dialisis disposes of both propositions without paradox (You say Jack loves to live, that brother Jules / Lives to love? Then I say both are fools: / One must be alive to love at any cost. / Then live to live, love love, or *all* is lost).

Ecphonesis is exclamation or outcry ("Forget that fool, my love," I scoffed, / "Soon we shall wed! / Soon we shall wed!").

Epithonema is climactic summation at the conclusion of a poem, a *coda* (from *cauda*, a tail), often in a single line or a couplet, as in the English SONNET.

Epitropis is used when the speaker believes he or she has said enough and refers the reader to something else to complete the thought (I've said enough. Time for another beer. / You take these definitions on from here).

Erotema is the *rhetorical question,* a question for which no answer is given or expected because, in context, the answer is obvious, as in the example illustrating asteismus.

Etiologia is the argumentative technique of assigning a cause or reason for an action or a circumstance:

> Take next,
> for thy next mistake
> (for muckrake you must
> once you've begun to raise dust,
> for, to settle the dust,
> to everyone be fair
> or unfair rather, without care,
> that is, care less rather than more
> how you effect your cure,
> you must sprinkle dews
> on the dust, not as you choose,
> but as you list, . . .)*

Ironia, or *irony,* is witty mockery, usually effected by saying the opposite of what is actually meant (The lover, intent on camping, went / Into the woods with the best in tent). In this case, the irony depends upon a pun on the word "intent."

Meiosis is a method of irony or sarcasm that diminishes the importance of something, "He's a big man indeed—big-headed and big-bellied."

Metanoia makes a statement, then retracts it by substituting something else (They tell me that your head is filled with stone. / O, surely not! But maybe solid bone).

Micterismus is verbal sneering (The old professor knows that books are safe. / He knows he's really Samson on the make, / Too smart to lose his eyes).

Noema is an ironic way of speaking by saying one thing on the surface but meaning something quite different, "You say Fred lives his life without a taint? / You're right. I wish to God he were a saint." On the surface, the speaker agrees with the appraisal of Fred, but in fact he wishes Fred were dead, as only the dead can be saints.

Orismus gives a definition different from someone else's definition of a word or phrase:

The school's a madhouse? Nay,
a bedroom, maybe, . . .*

Paralepsis makes little of something by passing over it lightly or denying it is of importance, thereby emphasizing its actual importance through understatement:

and here is *All America:*
what's there to say of him?
He has a pretty wife.
He keeps his hair in trim.*

Paramalogia is, in George Puttenham's words, "the figure of admittance." It admits arguments to the contrary so as to undercut the opponent's case:

Oh, what a mess
is this paper. I guess
poor Bod's hopeless. I am unlettered,
sirs, a man fettered
by ignorance. Ignore,

if you will, my bespattered
page, for I've been but smattered
with lore here and there.
Beware
the dull pen, sirs—it may tell lies
or, worse, my lords, truth,
if you watch not your way.*

Parimia is to speak by means of proverbs ("An apple a day keeps the doctor away." / That's true—he'd rather have money as pay).

Parisia is an apology by the writer of scurrilous or, as Puttenham says, "licentious" material:

Sirs,
I am one of your proslers,
no poet. In prose
anything goes.
Not so in verse,
or so they converse
in the various schools.
I would beg to disagree,
if it were not that fools
such as yours truly
tend toward the unruly,
which is why there are rules.*

Procatalepsis preempts opposing arguments by anticipating the argument before the opponent can articulate it:

We ought to break
into breakneck
Skeltonics just about now,
Gentlemen, I know, but perhaps
we'll just let the meters break down
a tiny bit.*

Sarcasmus, or *sarcasm,* is heavy irony or, as Puttenham described it, "the bitter taunt." There is little wit in sarcasm, as, for instance, when one bridge partner says to the other who has just played a bad hand, "Oh, you're just a terrific player, simply marvelous."

Tapinosis is saying too little about a subject—understatement. It is not the same, however, as *litotes* (see the next chapter) or studied understatement. The heart of poetry is saying just enough. Frequently, a poet is more effective by merely showing the situation—letting it speak for itself—rather than telling the reader how to think or feel about a subject.

5　The Ideational Level

A poem is an artifice of thought as well as of metrics, sonics, and tropes, and there is no thought except in symbols, in forms. Every element of language is a form of some kind. The letters of the alphabet are forms—conventions, the meanings of which we have agreed upon in order to communicate. Syllables are forms, as are words, phrases, and sentences. The poet is interested in all of these forms, since his or her medium is language. On the ideational level, we deal with the subject of words, specifically in their grammatic and syntactic forms.

ORTHOGRAPHICAL SCHEMAS

Orthographical schemas are about single words and syllables.

Prosthesis adds syllables at the beginning of a word *without changing the meaning of that word* (i.e., "configuration" for "figuration").

Proparalepsis adds syllables at the end of a word (i.e., "figuration" for "figure").

Epenthis adds syllables in the center of a word (i.e., "disenfigure" for "disfigure").

Aphaeresis is an overt elision technique that drops the initial, unstressed syllable of a word, usually a vowel (i.e., "'til" for "until," "'tis" for "it is," "let's" for "let us").

Apocope drops syllables from the end of a word ("morn" for "morning"—see *apocopated rhyme*).

Syncope is an overt elision technique that drops a syllable from the center of a word (i.e., "suff'ring" for "suffering").

Synalepha is an overt elision technique wherein one of two adjacent, unaccented vowels is suppressed to achieve the effect of only one unaccented syllable (i.e., "Th'art of poetic diction").

Hyphaeresis is an overt elision technique that drops a *consonant* from the center of a word in order to telescope two syllables and make them one, as in "whene'er" for "whenever." Note that aphaeresis, apocope, hyphaeresis, synalepha, and syncope are methods of contraction. For more information on this subject, see *elision* in chapter 3.

Amphisbaenia turns a word backward to make another word, as in "He *mined* ore in *denim* cloth" (see *amphisbaenic rhyme*).

Anagram is a word, phrase, or sentence constructed by rearranging (*transposing*) the letters of another word, phrase, or sentence: "live" = "vile," "stunted" = "student." *Metathesis* transposes the letters of a word; it is the process of forming an anagram. (See the section on the ANAGRAM in Part II.)

Antisthecon changes the sound of a word; for instance, "stoont" for "student."

Diaeresis concerns the pronunciation of two contiguous vowels in different ways (i.e., "Coöperation," "neologism").

Dialect changes the spelling of a word, but not its sound, "vittles" for "victuals," "parlour" for "parlor," or "Chumley" for "Cholmondelay" (see *dialect rhyme*).

Homographs (*homomorphs*) are words spelled alike but with totally different meanings, such as the verb bore, "to drill," and the noun bore, "a dull person." *Homographic rhyme* is a form of *rime riche*.

Homonyms are words that sound alike but that are spelled differently and have different meanings (bear - bare, time - thyme). *Homonymic rhyme* is a form of *rime riche*. While we are speaking of "rhyme," it might be well to note that the correct spelling of the word is, in fact, "rime" or the Middle English "ryme." Because of confusion over the centuries with the word *rhythm,* from the Greek *rhythmos* and Latin *rhythmus,* the orthographic form has, in common English usage, been corrupted.

A *palindrome* is a word, phrase, clause, or larger unit that reads the same backwards as forward: "radar" = "radar"; "Able was I ere I saw Elba" = "Able was I ere I saw Elba."

Tmesis is the breaking up of a compound word, usually by inserting a related word (i.e., "when you ever go" instead of "whenever you go"). This technique was used by the twentieth-century poet e. e. cummings.

CONSTRUCTIONAL SCHEMAS

Constructional schemas have to do with the ways in which words, phrases, clauses, and larger units are grammatically balanced. *Grammatical parallelism* was discussed when I talked about prose prosodies. *Synonymia* is paraphrase in parallel structures (I love you; you are my beloved); *synthesis* is consequence in parallel structures (I love you; therefore, I am yours); *antithesis* is the opposition of ideas expressed in parallel structures (I love you, and I loathe you); *auxesis* is the building up, in parallel structures, of a catalog or series that ultimately closes at the *zenith* (high point) of the set (the *climax:* I love your eyes, hair, breasts; I love the way you walk and speak; I love you); *meiosis* is the building down, in parallel structures, of a catalog or series that ultimately closes at the *nadir* (low point) of the set (the *anticlimax:* We struggled through dense forests; we forded raging torrents; we battled the terrors of storm and starvation to reach the road; we took the bus home). Kenneth Fearing's "Dirge" in *Poetry* (op. cit.) is an example.

Chiasmus is cross-parallelism in parallel structures:

> *I vied with the wind,* she fought the air,
> and as she lost, *I was victorious.*

Syneciosis cross-couples *antonyms,* words antithetical in meaning or opposite in such a way as to make them agree: "We are ourselves *victim* and *victor.* / You were and are ourselves." The italicized words are the antonyms. See "November 22, 1963" in *Poetry* (op. cit.) for an example of syneciosis.

Isocolon is a term that designates *perfect parallelism* (see *isoverbal prosody* in chapter 3). *Brachiologa* is the technique of separating words by pauses, usually indicated by means of punctuation (commas in particular) but sometimes typographically by means of spaces, as in the original version of Ezra Pound's "A Station of the Metro" (in *Poetry: An Introduction* [op. cit.]) or as in James Dickey's poem "Falling" in *The New Yorker Book of Poems* (New York, 1969).

Parison is construction using parallel clauses of equal weight, as in Chidiock Tichborne's "Elegy," written during the English Renaissance on the evening of his execution:

Elegy: On The Evening of His Execution

My prime of youth is but a frost of cares,
My feast of joy is but a dish of pain,
My crop of corn is but a field of tares,
And all my good is but vain hope of gain;
The day is past, and yet I saw no sun,
And now I live, and now my life is done.

My tale was heard and yet it was not told,
My fruit is fallen, and yet my leaves are green,
My youth is spent and yet I am not old,
I saw the world and yet I was not seen;
My thread is cut and yet it is not spun,
And now I live, and now my life is done.

I sought my death and found it in my womb,
I looked for life and saw it was a shade,
I trod the earth and knew it was my tomb,
And now I die, and now I was but made;
My glass is full, and now my glass is run,
And now I live, and now my life is done.

—CHIDIOCK TICHBORNE

This poem illustrates both parallel constructions and the trope of paradox, for each pair of clauses contains an inherent contradiction which finally, nevertheless, is true. It also illustrates *sinathrismus,* "the heaping figure" in Puttenham's parlance or, as it is now called, the "catalog," a listing of things in parallel. A well-known poem that illustrates sinathrismus is Carl Sandburg's "Chicago."

SYNTAX

Syntax is word order in a sentence. Donald Davie in his book *Articulate Energy* (New York, 1958) discusses the various types of syntax found in poetry. For consistency here, Davie's terminology will at times be changed.

Davie says that "Poetic syntax is [*egopoetic*] when its function is to please us by the fidelity with which [word order] follows the 'form of thought' in the poet's mind." In other words, the poet chooses a word order that tells the reader exactly what he is thinking, as in the first line of the eighteenth-century poet Christopher Smart's poem "The Coffin, the Cradle, and the Purse": "For the coffin and the cradle and the purse are all against a man." Egopoetic syntax is *subjective word order,* personal opinion:

I'm Nobody

I'm nobody! Who are you?
Are you nobody, too?
Then there's a pair of us—don't tell!
They'd banish us, you know.

How dreary to be somebody!
How public, like a frog
To tell your name the livelong day
To an admiring bog.
　　　—EMILY DICKINSON

Davie says, "Poetic syntax is [*narrative*] when the function is to please us by the fidelity with which [word order] follows a 'form of action,' a movement not through any mind, but in the world at large," as in this poem based on lines from Emily Dickinson's letters:

The Naked Eye

　　The chickens grow very fast—
　I am afraid they will be so large
　　that you cannot perceive them
　with the naked eye when you get home.

　　The flowers have reached the eaves
　and are heaving against the roof
　　which has begun to buckle—
　you will have to do something I fear.

We had eggs for breakfast or,
rather, an egg—the yellow yolk
ran under the sideboard, and
it stayed there, refusing to come out.

The cat walking down the stair
makes a great noise—the banister
bulges out as she descends.
The trees in the yard block out the sun—

we are not sure that the sun
still regards us in our small world
with a great eye fully clothed
in the raiment of its rays and beams.

We stumble in the shadows.
The candles speak so slightly that
we can hardly hear their words,
and the moss—the moss is at the door.

Davie writes, "Poetic syntax is *dramatic* when its function is to please us by the fidelity with which it follows the 'form of thought' in some mind other than the poet's, which the poet imagines." This word order is the same as egopoetic, except that it tells us not what is in the mind of the poet, but what is in the mind of an imaginary character—the thoughts of a *persona:*

Dying

I heard a fly buzz when I died;
    The stillness round my form
Was like the stillness in the air
    Between the heaves of storm.

The eyes beside had wrung them dry,
    And breaths were gathering sure
For that last onset, when the king
    Be witnessed in his power.

I willed my keepsakes, signed away
    What portion of me I

Could make assignable—and then
   There interposed a fly,

With blue, uncertain, stumbling buzz,
   Between the light and me;
And then the windows failed, and then
   I could not see to see.
            —EMILY DICKINSON

At first glance, this poem might seem to be written in ego-poetic syntax. Hyatt H. Waggoner in his book *American Poets from the Puritans to the Present* (Boston, 1968), however, pointed out that Nathaniel Hawthorne was one of Dickinson's favorite authors, and that this poem is, in fact, written from the viewpoint of the persona of Judge Pyncheon in *The House of the Seven Gables,* at the moment of his death as he sat in front of a window. A moment's thought would perhaps have led us to realize that the speaker is dead, and that one cannot speak from beyond the grave under ordinary circumstances. These three kinds of poetic syntax are traditional, and they are easily understood, but not so with the fourth sort.

According to Davie, "Poetic syntax is [*abstract*] when its function is to please us by the fidelity with which it follows a 'form of thought' through the poet's mind *but without defining that thought.*"

Bloom upon the Mountain

Bloom upon the Mountain—stated—
Blameless of a Name—
Efflorescence of a Sunset—
Reproduced—the same

Seed, had I, my Purple Sowing
Should endow the Day—
Not a Tropic of a Twilight—
Show itself away—

Who for tilling—to the Mountain
Come, and disappear—

Who be Her Renown, or fading,
Witness, is not here—

While I state—the Solemn Petals,
Far as North—and East,
Far as South and West—expanding—
Culminate—in Rest—

And the Mountain to the Evening
Fit His Countenance—
Indicating, by no Muscle—
The Experience—

—EMILY DICKINSON

Music is the most abstract of the arts because there are no
conventional meanings attached to notes as there are to
words. Some twentieth-century painters chose to jettison
representational figures in order to approximate music, and
the result was "abstract" art. Similarly, if a poet strips words
of their denotations and uses them for their connotations
only, the poet is then writing in abstract syntax (see much of
the work of Wallace Stevens and John Ashbery and the just
quoted poem by Emily Dickinson). In any particular poem,
a poet might, of course, mix two or more kinds of poetic
syntax.

Hyperbaton is the term that indicates the various kinds of
dislocation or inversion of grammatic syntax:

Anastrophe is the inversion of normal word order ("Go I shall"
for "I shall go"). *Cacosintheton* is anastrophe misused, as in an ar-
tificial "poetic diction" (more about *diction* later).

Hypallage is an exchange of words in phrases or clauses. The
technique is used in the first line of e. e. cummings' poem "Anyone
Lived in a Pretty How Town." The title is also the first line of the
poem, and it can be read in these ways: "anyone lived in a pretty
how town," "anyone lived in how pretty a town," or "how anyone
lived in a pretty town." The third version is normal syntactic order
as part of a longer sentence, for instance, "How anyone lived in a
pretty town is beyond me."

Parenthesis is the insertion of material that interrupts the thought

(I was going—or have I told you this?—to go away). A prosody—parenthetics—based on this schema is discussed in *Poetry* (op. cit.). *Epitheton* (apposition) is an inserted, synonymous modification of a sentence element, such as a subject (John Jones, *my good friend,* is a poet).

Anacoluthon is a shift of grammatical construction in midsentence that leaves the beginning unfinished (You may remember the night—listen! The dog is barking at the door).

Hendiadys is a construction that treats a double subject or object as though it were singular, not plural, in order to express a thought that is operating on more than one level (My lust and her adamance is Hell).

Hysteron proteron is the reversal of chronological events for purposes of intensification or stress ("Let us break our necks and jump" rather than "Let us jump and break our necks").

Zeugma (to be distinguished from *zeugmatic syllepsis*) is a yoking or binding together of two sentence elements by means of another element, which would otherwise have had to be repeated elsewhere in the sentence. Three kinds of zeugma have been distinguished: *prozeugma,* in which the binding element precedes the parts it binds, "*Everyone* wishes to come, and [everyone] will do so, regardless"; *mesozeugma,* in which the binding element is between the yoked parts, "This is the place *he loved,* and the woman [he loved]"; *hypozeugma,* in which the binding element follows the yoked parts, "Neither life [need be feared], nor death itself *need be feared.*"

EXCLUSIVE AND INCLUSIVE SCHEMAS

Exclusive schemas are constructions that leave things out of the sentence:

Ellipsis leaves out words, thereby speaking in a starker way than is normal, as in "I love the dark" rather than "I am in love with darkness." Ellipsis is an essential part of the HAIKU.

Asyndeton, the opposite of *polysyndeton,* eliminates articles, conjunctions, and sometimes prepositions and pronouns from normal sentences (I chased [the] wind, [the] wind chased me).

Aposiopesis is the simple deletion of an important letter, syllable, word, or passage (You can go to ----!).

Syllepsis includes two kinds: *Elliptical syllepsis* is a grammatical construction in which one part of speech controls two other elements, agreeing with only one of them (She *kisses* me, and I [kiss] her); *zeugmatic syllepsis* has a part of speech correctly controlling two other elements, but controlling them in different ways (He *waited* with *mind* and *dagger* sharp).

Inclusive schemas add things to the sentence:

Enallage changes the tense, gender, or number of some part of speech. This construction is rare in English. For an example, see the poem titled "The Guestroom" in *Poetry: An Introduction* (op. cit.).

Irmus is suspended sense. Not until the end of a passage does the reader fully understand what is being spoken of (see Morton Marcus' poem titled "Look Closely" in his collection *Where the Oceans Cover Us* [Santa Barbara, 1972]).

Merismus expands upon a subject by particularizing each element of it. Bill Sloan's poem "A Portrait of the Day," found in Alberta Turner's *Poets Teaching* (op. cit.), is based upon this schema as well as the next construction, prolepsis.

Prolepsis expands upon a general statement, particularizing it and giving further information regarding it, as in Tichborne's "Elegy" quoted previously.

SUBSTITUTIVE AND REPETITIVE SCHEMAS

Substitutive schemas replace sentence elements with others.

Anthimeria substitutes one part of speech for another—for example, a noun for a verb in "The clock's chime *belfries* over the town," or as in d. a. levy's "Bop for Kiddies" where the narrator says, "i *watermeloned* down the lawn" (see *Poetry: An Introduction* [op. cit.] for further discussion of this poem).

Antonomasia substitutes for a noun a phrase describing the noun. The descriptive phrase is derived from some quality associated with the noun. For instance, instead of saying "Queen Elizabeth I," a poet might (and often does) say, "The Virgin Queen." A trope that utilizes antonomasia is the *kenning*.

Hyperbole is calculated exaggeration (Her eyes were as big as moons), as in Kenneth Fearing's "Dirge" cited previously.

Implied aposiopesis substitutes another letter, syllable, word, or passage for the dropped material (You are an as-*phyxiating* person).

Litotes, the reverse of hyperbole, is studied understatement, as in John Crowe Ransom's "Bells for John Whiteside's Daughter" where the poet uses the term "brown study"—a faraway look in the eyes, an unfocused look—as a substitute for the glazed look of death.

Metalepsis substitutes for a word a synonym that is essentially metaphorical since the equation between the word and its synonym is not obvious—for instance, "I met Ray just as he first thumbed / the last of thirteen buttons," instead of "I met Ray on the day he enlisted in the Navy." Out of context, the line seems farfetched. In a way, it *is* farfetched, and, in fact, Puttenham called this structure the *farfet*, a neologism. For the poem "Ray," see "The Sketches" in my *Pocoangelini: A Fantography* (Northampton, 1971).

Metonymy is a way of describing by using a word related to a word rather than the original word itself ("The *heart* will find a way" rather than "*Love* will find a way").

Paradiastole substitutes for a word an antonym rather than a synonym, to ironic effect. For instance, when speaking of a cheap skate you might say, "Skinflint is *generous* to a fault," or, of a coward, "He *bravely* rose in battle and ran away."

Periphrasis is saying something in a more grandiloquent or roundabout way than is usual—"She was taken unto the bosom of her forebears" rather than "She died."

Prosonomasia is a way of nicknaming someone by substituting a letter or letters in his name, thereby describing him by some personal characteristic. For instance, if a very thin man were named "Jones," you might substitute a *B* for the *J* and call him "Bones."

Synecdoche describes by substituting a part for the whole, as in "He was the King's legs" rather than "He was the King's messenger."

Repetitional schemas are reiterative constructions.

Anadiplosis is the linking of two consecutive verses or stanzas by repeating words (I saw her hair, / Her dark *hair* windblown).

Anaphora is the parallel repetition of a beginning word or phrase in succeeding lines of verse:

Of the Spiritual Musick

For the spiritual musick is as follows.

For there is the Thunder-Stop, which is the voice of God
    direct.

For the rest of the Stops are by their rhimes.

For the Trumpet rhimes are sound bound, soar more and the
    like.

For the Shawm rhimes are lawn fawn moon boon and the like.

For the Harp rhimes are sing ring, string & the like.

For the Cymbal rhimes are bell well toll soul & the like.

For the Flute rhimes are tooth youth suit mute & the like.

For the Dulcimer rhimes are grace place beat heat & the like.

For the Clarinet rhimes are clean seen and the like.

For the Bassoon rhimes are pass, class and the like. God be
    gracious to Baumgarden.

For the Dulcimer are rather van fan & the like and grace place
    &c are of the Bassoon.

For beat heat, weep peep &c are of the Pipe.

For every word has its marrow in the English tongue for order
    and for delight.

For the dissyllables such as able, table &c are the Fiddle rhimes.

For all dissyllables and some trissyllables are Fiddle rhimes.

For the relations of words are sometimes in oppositions.

For the relations of words are according to their distances from
    the pair.

—CHRISTOPHER SMART

Antanaclasis is the witty repetition of a word in an amplified or
changed sense, that is, the *pun*:

Eve's Daughter

Eve's daughter can entrance you with her eyes;
Her hisses and her curves can mesmerize.
Fellows, be wary of her. Shun the snake.
To do a Serpent in you need a *Rake*.

—WESLI COURT

Antanaclasis is one of Empson's forms of ambiguity, discussed
previously.

Antimetabole is the repetition of two beginning words, in reverse order, later in a verse or sentence (To *kiss her* is to love *her kiss*).

Antistrophe repeats a single word throughout a poem, particularly an end-word, as in the Smart poem just quoted or the French SESTINA.

Echoics were discussed under the sonic level.

Emphasis reinforces a word. It can be done in several ways—by repetition (He was dumb, dumb, dumb!); by using a different typeface such as italics (He was *dumb!*); by building a series of synonyms (He was dumb—I mean, he was ignorant, stupid, and otherwise thick), and so forth.

Epanalepsis is the repetition of a word, for clarity or for emphasis, after the intervention of a word, phrase, or clause. In verse, epanalepsis specifically means to end a line, stanza, or poem with the same word or words with which it began. The Irish bards called this construction *dunadh* (dóo-na), and certain forms, such as the RONDEAU and the ROUNDEL require this kind of repetition.

Epanodis, like prolepsis, expands upon a general statement, but in addition, it repeats terms contained *in* the general statement.

Epimone is the term meaning the use of repeated lines at intervals within a poem, discussed in the chapter on the sonic level under "refrain."

Epiphora is the repetition of end-words or end-phrases specifically, as in the SESTINA.

Epizeuxis repeats a word without any pause between (Tramp, tramp, tramp, the boys are marching).

Hypozeuxis is the repetition of words in parallel constructions. The repeated words govern the sense of the clause or clauses of which they are a part (Up to *the door* I'll go, and at *the door* I'll rap, / Whether or not the man I seek is lying in his nap).

Ploce is the repetition of words or phrases at irregular intervals throughout a stanza, poem, or long passage.

Polyptoton is the repetition of words derived from the same root (He *ran,* will *run,* and is *running* now).

Polysyndeton is the repetition of conjunctions—the opposite of asyndeton (see *exclusive schemas*)—and is to be distinguished from *anaphora.*

Symploce is a combination of anaphora or antistrophe and epiphora.

DICTION AND VOICE

I have noted that syntax deals with the order of words in a sentence. In contemporary speech, the following would be an example of normal word order or syntax: "A thought of grief came to me alone." In this sentence, the subject comes first, then the predicate: "A thought . . . came . . . to me. . . ." In line four of stanza three from Wordsworth's "Ode," cited previously, the normal syntax is changed: "To me alone there came a thought of grief." The two sentences say exactly the same thing, but they *sound* different because of the syntax, which has transformed *the level of diction* in the line. The tone of the second version has been "elevated," and it is now an example of *poetic diction,* a diction designed specifically for writing what nineteenth-century poets considered to be an appropriately "elevated" poetry.

Syntax and diction are related. They depend on one another, but they are not the same thing. Syntax is concerned with the *form* of the sentence; diction has to do with its *tone* and *style.* The level of diction of a truck driver is different (usually) from that of an archbishop. An archbishop speaks in an elevated "style," a truck driver, perhaps, in an idiomatic style. These styles are dependent on the levels of diction the individuals choose to speak in.

A truck driver in a play could not say, "To me alone there came a thought of grief," because the sentence would not be in character; the level of diction is poetic, not vernacular. To be believable as a character, the truck driver would have to say something like, "A sad thought came to me by my lonesome." The level of diction would thus be in keeping with the character, and the sentence would be an example of *base* style rather than *mean* or *high* style.

If an older, well-educated woman character was written into the script, a different version might fit: "A thought of grief came to me alone," an example of mean style. The archbishop might say, "To me alone there came a thought of grief"—high style and poetic diction. Only in this last version, however, is the word order, the syntax, out of normal order. It is "artificial" syntax; it does not seem "natural" but is perfectly good English.

Someone speaks in every poem ever written. There are three narrative voices, which parallel the three major and traditional syntaxes: the *egopoetic,* the *narrative,* and the *dramatic* voices. There are three persons and two numbers of voice: first, second, and third person speakers, and singular and plural numbers. This table will help us see who is speaking, and what he or she is speaking about:

Voice:	Egopoetic	Narrative	Dramatic
Person:			
First	I	I, we	I
Second		you, you (pl.)	
Third		he, she, it, they	

The egopoetic voice is single-angled. The speaker is taking a stance at the center of his or her world and telling about it from the first-person singular viewpoint. The egopoet's method is autobiographical in nature and exclusive in effect. There is but one angle of vision, and either the reader agrees with the poet or not. Those who do not agree are excluded from participation in the subjective, ego-centered relationship. Egopoets often use rhetorical methods, *telling* rather than *persuading* or *showing.* Most lyric poetry is written in the egopoetic voice, but traditionally the interest of the poem is carried by the music of the poem, by the sonic level which makes it palatable.

The narrative voice is double-angled at least, depending on the number of characters whose stories are being told in the poem. The poet relates someone else's or perhaps his own story by *standing outside* himself or herself and taking an objective viewpoint. The reader is not excluded by the narration because he or she is encouraged to *empathize,* at least with the *protagonist*—the lead character. By the way the poet tells the story, there is also an inclusive *angle of reflection* that tells us as much about the narrator, perhaps, as about the character in the poem. More information about narrative viewpoint will be found in the section on NARRATIVES.

The dramatic voice is similar to the narrative voice, except that here the poet takes the reader *inside* another character's person, and both we and the poet *become* that person. We therefore see the persona's world in the same way that we saw the poet's world from the egopoetic viewpoint. The main difference is that we can still see the poet-speaker's viewpoint by reflection, as in the narrative voice, from the way in which the poet makes the persona speak. The dramatic viewpoint is the most inclusive of the three, for it is both objective and "subjective" (from the viewpoint of the character). The more personae the poet imagines in the poem the more inclusive it is.

All three viewpoints and voices can be blended in a work of literature, and the effect is potentially "universal." For example, both Dante and Chaucer not only told great stories about other people in the *Divine Comedy* and *The Canterbury Tales,* respectively, but also included themselves in their stories as characters, and had their various personae tell their own stories as well. Here is another table, showing correspondences among the major and minor subgenres of the genre of poetry, the three traditional syntaxes, and the three voices:

Major subgenres	Traditional syntaxes	Voices
Lyrics (songs)	Egopoetic	Egopoetic
Narratives (stories)	Narrative	Narrative
Dramatics (speeches)	Dramatic	Dramatic

Minor subgenres	Traditional syntaxes	Voices
Bucolics (pastorals)	Dramatic	Dramatic
Didactics (lessons)	Egopoetic/ narrative	Egopoetic/ narrative
Forensics (debates)	Dramatic	Dramatic
Occasionals (memorials)	Egopoetic	Egopoetic
Satirics (mockery/ parody)	Narrative	Narrative

There is but one element left to discover: What is the *theme* of the poem under consideration? If the subject can be stated in a single word or phrase, for instance "love," what has the poet said about love? The theme is stated *only* in a complete sentence: "Love is a many-splintered thing" perhaps, or "Love is an abstraction that can be defined in as many ways as there are individuals on the earth."

11 The New Book of Forms

6 Form-Finder Index

Every element of language is a form of some kind, as I have suggested at earlier points; but there are certain structures that have traditionally been associated with the genre of poetry, and these will be the subject of the rest of this volume. Over three hundred of these forms are listed here. To identify the form of a poem, the reader should first determine its *meter;* second, determine its *rhyme scheme;* third, count the lines in one *stanza* (if looking for a stanza form) or the lines in the whole poem (if looking for a poem form). When these elements have been determined, the reader should look under the appropriate heading of the following Form-Finder: if the form is irregular, look under *General Forms;* if the form is regular, look under *Specific Forms* and then under the appropriate subheading ("One-Line Forms" through "Two Hundred Ten-Line Forms"). Under these headings are the lists of forms. Definitions of all these forms are listed alphabetically in the next chapter. The poem in question can be compared with the appropriate definitions until the form of that poem or stanza has been found.

One final note: many poems are "regular," that is, traditionally formal, but the specific combinations of stanza pattern, line lengths, rhyme schemes, and meters have been created by the poet. Such poems are called *nonce forms.*

SPECIFIC FORMS

One-Line Forms
adonic (see SAPPHICS)
Alexandrine (see POULTER'S MEASURE)
Anglo-Saxon Prosody
blank verse (see *Sonics,* p. 27 and HEROICS)

choriambics
classical hexameter (see ELEGIACS)
  classical pentameter
cyhydedd naw ban
fourteener (see POULTER'S MEASURE)
grammatic parallels (see *Prose prosodies*, p. 8)
  antithetical parallel   synonymous parallel
  climactic parallel   synthetic parallel
hendecasyllabics
heroic line (see HEROICS)
hudibrastics (see SATIRICS)
mondo (see KATAUTA)
mote
rhupunt
Sapphic line (see SAPPHICS)
septenary (see POULTER'S MEASURE)
tawddgyrch cadwynog (see RHUPUNT)

Two-Line Forms

barzeletta
carol texte
choka
couplet
  Alexandrine couplet
  cyhydedd fer
  cywydd deuair fyrion
  cywydd deuair hirion
  Nashers
  qasida
  short couplet
  split couplet

elegiacs
heroic couplet (see HEROICS)
Hudibrastics (see SATIRICS)
Nasher (see PROSE POEMS)
Poulter's measure
primer couplet (see DIDACTICS)
tanka couplet (see TANKA)

Three-Line Forms

blues stanza
haiku
  hokku
  senryu
katauta
  (see FORENSICS)

tercet
  enclosed tercet
  Sicilian tercet
terza rima
  capitolo

triplet
  enclosed triplet
  englyn milwr
  englyn penfyr
  Sicilian triplet
triversen stanza

Six-Line Forms

clogyrnach
cywydd llosgyrnog
gwawdodyn hir
   (see GWAWDODYNS)
hir a thoddaid
rime couée
  standard habbie

sestet
  heroic sestet
  Italian sestet
  sextilla
  Sicilian sestet
short particular measure
somonka
stave
  couplet envelope

Seven-Line Forms

rime royal
rondelet

septet
  Sicilian septet

Eight-Line Forms

ballade stanza
  double ballade stanza
  double refrain ballade stanza
  huitain
common octave
  (see COMMON MEASURE)
  hymnal octave
  long hymnal octave
  long octave
  short hymnal octave
  short octave
cyhydedd hir

cyrch a chwta
lai nouveau (see LAI)
madrigal
octave
  Italian octave
  Sicilian octave
  strambotto
ottava rima
rispetto
  heroic octave
  heroic rispetto
triolet

Nine-Line Forms

lai
  virelai
Ronsardian ode stanza

Spenserian stanza
triad (see TERCET)

Ten-Line Forms

ballade supreme stanza
  dizain
  double ballade supreme stanza

decastich
English ode stanza (see ODE)
madrigal

Twenty-Eight-Line Forms
ballade
   double refrain ballade

Thirty-Line Forms
English ode (see ODE)

Thirty-Five-Line Forms
ballade supreme (see BALLADE)

Thirty-Nine-Line Forms
sestina

Forty-Eight-Line Forms
double ballade (see BALLADE)

Sixty-Line Forms
chant royal
double ballade supreme (see BALLADE)

Ninety-Eight-Line Forms
crown of sonnets (see SONNET)

Two Hundred-Line Forms
qasida

Two Hundred Ten-Line Forms
sonnet redoubled (see SONNET)

GENERAL FORMS

acrostic
   double acrostic
   telestich
alba
allegory
anacreontics
anagram

antiphon
aubade
balada (see LYRICS)
   dansa
ballad
beast epic
bestiary

grammatics
  catalog
  parenthetics
  polyphonic prose
  prose poem
heroics
hokku
homostrophic ode (see ODE)
Horatian ode (see ODE)
idyl
incantation
interlude
irregular ode (see ODE)
katauta
lament
lay
litany
liturgics
  antiphon
  blessing
  canticle
  carol
  chant
  curse
  dirge (see LYRICS)
  evensong
  hymn (see LYRICS)
  incantation
  litany
  morningsong
  nightsong
  obsequy
  prayer
  sermon
lyrics
  alba (aubade)
  anacreontics
  balada
  blues
  caccia, catch

lyrics cont.
  canso, canzo, canzone
  carol
  chantey
  complaint
  dithyramb
  ditty
  elegy (coronach, dirge, monody, threnod
  encomium
  epithalamion, epithalamium
  hymn
  lament
  lay
  madrigal
  madsong
  nonsense verse
  nursery rhyme
  paean
  panegyric
  pastoral (idyl)
  pastoral elegy
  prothalamion, prothalamium
  reveille
  romance
  roundelay
  rune
  serenade
  sirvente
madrigal
madsong
mask, masque
metrical romance
miracle play
mondo
monody
monologue
morality play
morningsong
mote
mystery play

narratives
  ballad
  beast epic
  chanson de geste
  epic
  epyllion
  exemplum
  fabliau
nightsong
noh play (see DRAMATICS)
nonsense verse
nursery rhyme
obsequy
occasionals
  elegy
  epithalamion, epithalamium
  genethliacum
  obsequy
  ode
  palinode
  prothalamion, prothalamium
  triumphal ode
ode
  homostrophic ode
  irregular (Cowleyan) ode
  Pindaric ode
palinode
panegyric
passion play
pastoral, pastorale
pastoral elegy
pastoral ode

pastourelle
pattern verse
picture poem
Pindaric ode (see ODE)
plampede
posies
pregunta
prose poem
prothalamion, prothalamium
reveille
riddle
rimas dissolutas
romance
rune
satirics
  epigram
  epitaph
  sirvente (see LYRICS)
  Skeltonics
serenade
sermon
sirima
sirvente
Skeltonics
song (see LYRICS)
spatials
  calligramme
  concrete poem
telestich
tragedy
tragicomedy
tumbling verse

All these forms are listed alphabetically, with cross-references, in the succeeding pages.

7   The Forms of Poetry

ACROSTIC

Can be in any verse prosody or in any form, but is usually metered and rhymed. The first letters of all the lines, when read downward, spell out a word or a phrase, usually a name. The poem "To My Cousin, Mistress Ellinor Evins" provides an example. Note that the two words in the name form separate stanzas:

lines	verse
1.	E re I forget the zenith of your love,
2.	L et me be banished from the Thrones above;
3.	L ight let me never see, when I grow rude,
4.	I ntomb your love in base ingratitude:
5.	N or may I prosper, but the state
6.	O f gaping Tantalus be my fate;
7.	R ather than I should thus preposterous grow,
8.	E arth would condemn me to her vaults below.
9.	V irtuous and noble, could my genius raise
10.	I mmortal anthems to your vestal praise,
11.	N one should be more laborious than I,
12.	S aint-like to canonize you to the sky.

—GEORGE ALSOP

The DOUBLE ACROSTIC form repeats this feat with the last letters of the lines as well, the TELESTICH, only with the last letters of the lines. The COMPOUND ACROSTIC spells out words down the left-hand margin, with something *different* down the right-hand one.

For a very complicated acrostic, see Edward Taylor's "Acrostic Love Poem to Elizabeth Fitch" in *Poetry: An Introduction* (op. cit.).

AE FREISLIGHE *(ay Frésh-lee)*

Irish. Syllabic. Since this form is the first Celtic one to be encountered in this chapter, a note is in order. Almost all the Irish and Welsh forms are complex systems of rhyme, alliteration, and consonance (see *cynghanedd* in the chapter on the sonic level under "echoics"). For the practical purpose of versification in English, it should be understood that the systems are most difficult to reproduce accurately in our language. It would therefore be as well for the poet attempting these forms to pay attention only to the rhyme scheme and syllabification. Thus, ae freislighe, simplified, is a QUATRAIN STANZA of seven syllable lines. Lines one (1) and three (3) rhyme in triple rhymes; lines two (2) and four (4) rhyme in double rhymes.

The *poem* (not the stanza) should end with the same first syllable, word, or line with which it begins. The technical term for this ending is *dunadh,* and it occurs in all the Gaelic forms.

The diagram thus looks like this:

lines	syllables and rhymes
1.	x x x x (x x a)
2.	x x x x x (x b)
3.	x x x x (x x a)
4.	x x x x x (x b)

Love Curse

What's love but a bobolink
Beating its voice on the air,
A morningsong robawink,
Wrack of sleep beyond repair?

What's love but a nematode,
The worm that gnaws its wee hole,
A minuscule episode
Restless to become the whole?

Love, love, let me mock you thrice
With catspaw, rue, and foxglove.
Basilisk and cockatrice
Know how to answer, "What's love?"
                —WESLI COURT

ALBA—*see* AUBADE.

ALCAICS

Greek. Quantitative accentual-syllabics. Unrhymed. A QUA-
TRAIN stanza. The first two lines consist of an acephalous
iamb, two trochees, and two dactyls, in that order; the third
line consists of an acephalous iamb and four trochees, in that
order; the fourth line is made of two dactyls followed by two
trochees:

lines	meters
1.	x xx xx xxx xxx
2.	x xx xx xxx xxx
3.	x xx xx xx xx
4.	xxx xxx xx xx

The first half of the following poem is written in alcaics,
the second half in HENDECASYLLABICS.

Milton: (Alcaics)

O mighty-mouth'd inventor of harmonies,
O skill'd to sing of Time or Eternity,
    God-gifted organ-voice of England,
        Milton, a name to resound for ages;
Whose Titan angels, Gabriel, Abdiel,
Starr'd from Jehovah's gorgeous armories,
    Tower, as the deep-domed empyrean
        Rings to the roar of an angel onset—
Me rather all that bowery loneliness,
The brooks of Eden mazily murmuring,

And bloom profuse and cedar arches
   Charm, as a wanderer out in ocean,
Where some refulgent sunset of India
Streams o'er a rich ambrosial ocean isle,
   And crimson-hued the stately palm-woods
     Whisper in odorous heights of even.

[Catullus]: (Hendecasyllabics)

O you chorus of indolent reviewers,
Irresponsible, indolent reviewers,
Look, I come to the test, a tiny poem
All composed in a metre of Catullus,
All in quantity, careful of my motion,
Like the skater on ice that hardly bears him,
Lest I fall unawares before the people,
Waking laughter in indolent reviewers.
Should I flounder awhile without a tumble
Thro' this metrification of Catullus,
They should speak to me not without a welcome,
All that chorus of indolent reviewers.
Hard, hard, hard is it, only not to tumble,
So fantastical is the dainty metre.
Wherefore slight me not wholly, nor believe me
Too presumptuous, indolent reviewers.
O blatant Magazines, regard me rather—
Since I blush to belaud myself a moment—
As some rare little rose, a piece of inmost
Horticultural art, or half coquette-like
Maiden, not to be greeted unbenignly.
                 —ALFRED TENNYSON

ALEXANDRINE

The alexandrine is a *line* of iambic hexameter verse:

line   *meter*
        ´ ´ ´ ´ ´ ´
1.   xx xx xx xx xx xx

For the uses of the alexandrine, see POULTER'S MEASURE and
SPENSERIAN STANZA.

ALEXANDRINE COUPLET—*see* COUPLET.

ALLEGORY—*see* DIDACTICS, FABLE, FABLIAU,
     NARRATIVES; *also see the chapter on the sensory level.*

ANACREONTICS—*see* LYRICS.

ANAGRAM

Sometimes associated with the acrostic or serving as the epigraph of other kinds of poems. The anagram is a word or phrase made by transposing the letters of a name, for example, Gerald Ford = forged lard. Popular in the seventeenth century and earlier, casting anagrams was a form of divining; that is, it was a means of foretelling the future of a person or of extracting the essence of his or her life or personality:

```
        MARY
ANA-         GRAM
      ARMY
```

> How well her name an *Army* doth present,
> In whom the *Lord of Hosts* did pitch his tent!
> —GEORGE HERBERT

ANGLO-SAXON PROSODY

Accentual. A *line* utilizing alliteration and stress. For a complete discussion of this form, see *accentual prosody* under "metrical prosodies" in chapter 3. See also *sprung rhythm*. For a form sometimes associated with Anglo-Saxon prosody, see the BOB AND WHEEL. For a related prosody, see *podics* (chapter 3); and for a related form, see EDDA MEASURES. For examples, see "The Mystery" in the section on LITURGICS, "The Magi Carol" in the BOB AND WHEEL, "Three Riddles from the Anglo-Saxon" in DIDACTICS, and "The Morbid Man Singing" on pp. 18–19.

ANTIPHON—*see* LITURGICS.

AUBADE—*see* LYRICS.

AWDL GYWYDD *(owdl gów-widd)*

Welsh. Syllabic. A QUATRAIN stanza of seven syllable lines. Lines two (2) and four (4) rhyme; lines one (1) and three (3) *cross-rhyme into* the third, fourth, or fifth *syllable* of lines two (2) and four (4). Here is a possible scheme for two stanzas of awdl gywydd:

lines	syllables and rhymes	lines	syllables and rhymes
1.	x x x x x x a	5.	x x x x x x d
2.	x x a x x x b	6.	x x x d x x e
3.	x x x x x x c	7.	x x x x x x f
4.	x x x x c x b	8.	x x x f x x e

Here is a modern version of a medieval poem cast into awdl gywydd:

Spring Song

Earthspring, the sweetest season,
Loud the birdsong, sprouts ripple,
Plough in furrow, ox in yoke,
Sea like smoke, fields in stipple.

Yet when cuckoos call from trees
I drink the lees of sorrow;
Tongue bitter, I sleep with pain—
No kin remain this morrow.

On mountain, mead, seaborne land,
Wherever man wends his way,
What path he take boots not,
He shall not keep from Christ's eye.
—ANONYMOUS

BALADA—*see* LYRICS.

BALLAD

Universal in the Western world. Folk ballads are written in podic prosody, literary ballads in accentual-syllabics. The BALLAD STANZA is $a^4b^3c^4b^3$; however, the ballad can be written in any meter and in many forms. It is usually rhymed, and internal rhyme is sometimes used. There is no fixed stanza or line-length, and it often has a refrain or burden. Meant to be sung, the ballad can be defined as a lyric verse narrative, for all ballads tell stories.

The folk ballad is traditional and anonymously written; the literary ballad is a composition by a known author. The former often manifests a phenomenon called "leaping and lingering," meaning that it skips from high point to high point, ignoring details of the narrative. The literary ballad, however, develops the whole narrative, including details and climaxes. For more information concerning the prosody of the folk ballad, see *podic prosody*. Here is a possible scheme for two stanzas of ballad with a refrain:

lines	meters	lines	meters
1.	x x x x x x x a	5.	x x x x x x d
2.	x x x x x b	6.	x x x x x b
3.	x x x x x x x x c	7.	x x x x x x x e
4.	x x x x x x B	8.	x x x x x B

The following are two ballads—the first a folk ballad, the second a literary ballad:

The Unquiet Grave

"The wind doth blow today, my love,
   And a few small drops of rain;
I never had but one true-love,
   In a cold grave she was lain.

"I'll do as much for my true-love
   As any young man may;
I'll sit and mourn all at her grave
   For a twelvemonth and a day."

The twelvemonth and a day being up,
   The dead began to speak:

"Oh, who sits weeping on my grave
  And will not let me sleep?"

"It is I, my love, sits on your grave,
  And will not let you sleep;
For I crave one kiss of your clay-cold lips,
  And that is all I seek."

"You crave one kiss of my clay-cold lips?
  But my breath smells earthy strong!
If you have one kiss of my clay-cold lips,
  Your time will not be long.

"'Tis down in yonder garden green,
  Love, where we used to walk—
The finest flower that ere was seen
  Is withered to a stalk.

"The stalk is withered dry, my love,
  So will our hearts decay;
So make yourself content, my love,
  Till God calls you away."

—ANONYMOUS

The Little Boy Lost

"Father, father, where are you going?
  O do not walk so fast!
Speak, father, speak to your little boy,
  Or else I shall be lost."

The night was dark, no father was there,
  The child was wet with dew;
The mire was deep, and the child did weep,
  And away the vapour flew.

—WILLIAM BLAKE

For related forms, see COMMON MEASURE. For other narrative forms, see the LAY and ROMANCE in the section on LYRICS, the EPIC in the section on HEROICS, and the FABLIAU among the NARRATIVES. For contemporary ballads, see *Strong Measures;* for other ballads, see *Poetry* (ops. cit.).

BALLADE

A French form. Syllabic. Lines can be of any *single* length, but are usually of eight or ten syllables; in English, often iambic tetrameter or pentameter. The twenty-eight lines are divided into three OCTAVE stanzas and one QUATRAIN half-stanza called the *envoi* or *envoy*. The ballade turns on three rhymes and is built on a refrain, which appears as the last line of each stanza and of the envoy.

Here is the scheme for the first stanza:

line	rhymes
1.	a
2.	b
3.	a
4.	b
5.	b
6.	c
7.	b
8.	C—*refrain*

The second stanza (lines nine through sixteen) and the third stanza (lines seventeen through twenty-four) are exactly the same—*the rhyme sounds do not change,* though the words can vary except in the refrain. Here is the scheme for the envoy:

25.	b
26.	c
27.	b
28.	C—*refrain*

The BALLADE SUPREME has thirty-five lines: three ten-line stanzas rhyming *ababbccdcD*, with an envoy of five lines rhyming *ccdcD*. The refrain appears as the last line of each stanza and of the envoy. Note that this form has four rhymes.

The DOUBLE BALLADE and the DOUBLE BALLADE SUPREME have six stanzas of eight and ten lines, respectively, and fol-

low the rhyme schemes of the ballade and the ballade su-
preme. An envoy is *optional;* if one is used, it is the same as in
the ballade and ballade supreme. The refrain usually appears
as the last line of each stanza and of the envoy; however,
Chaucer's ballade—which has been modernized—has a vari-
ant envoy:

Complaint to His Purse

To you, my purse—to no one else in sight—
　　I make complaint, for you're my lady dear!
I am so sorry now that you are light
　　For, certainly, you make such heavy cheer
　　I'd just as soon be laid upon my bier.
I throw myself upon your mercy, cry,
"Be heavy again, otherwise I may die!"

Grant me this day—lest it be turned to night—
　　Your blissful jingle ringing on the ear,
Or let me see your sunshine color bright:
　　Its yellowness has never owned a peer.
　　You are my life, heart's helmsman at the steer,
Queen of comfort and of good company.
Be heavy again, otherwise I may die!

Now, purse, that are to me my lifetime's light
　　And saviour (that is, down in this world here),
Help me get out of town with all your might,
　　Since you refuse to be my treasurer
　　(For I am shaved as close as any friar).
Yet, again, I pray unto your courtesy,
Be heavy again, otherwise I may die!

l'envoi [to the king]:
Oh, conqueror of British Albion,
Who by lineage and election
　　Be truly king, this song to you I send,
　　And you who may all our harms amend,
Take heed to this, my supplication!
　　　　　　　　　　　—GEOFFREY CHAUCER

Contemporary ballades by Ron Block, Dudley Randall, and Judith Johnson Sherwin can be found in *Strong Measures* (op. cit.).

The DOUBLE REFRAIN BALLADE has three, eight-line stanzas rhyming *abaBbcbC,* with an envoy of four lines rhyming *bBcC*. It also has two refrains. The first refrain appears as lines four, twelve, twenty, and twenty-six; the second refrain appears as lines eight, sixteen, twenty-four, and twenty-eight:

Will Somers
(*from* Bordello)

The sun shone all day
like a bright cock preening
for its hen. Making hay
lay over the greening
grass. There is no meaning
hidden for you to trace
in these wishes leaning
like moonlight on my face,

for I live as I may—
I, Will Somers—gleaning
in all weathers. I say,
"Lay over the greening
world well, the wind keening
or sighing." Woman's grace
is but a night's dreaming,
like moonlight on my face:

a thing met with on the way,
taken without scheming.
I never married. Clay
lay over the greening
sap of my youth. Steaming
nights I spent alone; lace
fancies all went streaming
like moonlight on my face,
like sweat. Sweat, careening,

lay over the greening
fields. Now, I know love's place,
like moonlight on my face.
                    —L. T.

The CHANT ROYAL, a member of the ballade family, is listed
separately. The HUITAIN is a complete poem composed of one
ballade stanza (*ababbcbc*). Huitains used as stanzas are some-
times called MONK'S TALE STANZA. The DIZAIN is a complete
poem composed of one ballade supreme stanza (*ababbccdcd*).
The lines for both the huitain and the dizain are either eight
or ten syllables in length or iambic tetrameter or pentameter
in accentual-syllabic prosody.

Note that the addition of an ALEXANDRINE line to the iam-
bic pentameter huitain to form a final couplet (*ababbcbcc⁶*)
will result in one SPENSERIAN STANZA.

BALLADE SUPREME—*see* BALLADE.

BALLAD STANZA—*see* BALLAD.

BARZELETTA
Italian. Written in COUPLETS having seven syllables in each
line, or in BLANK VERSE pentameters, heptameters, or hen-
decasyllabics. It uses internal rhyme and profuse aphorisms,
witticisms, and didacticisms.

BEAST EPIC, BESTIARY
Animal fables in verse or prose used as allegories of human
nature.

BLANK VERSE—*see* HEROICS.

BLUES SONNET—*see* BLUES STANZA.

BLUES STANZA
American. A TRIPLET stanza derived from the Black jazz tra-
dition of lamentation or complaint, rhyming *AAa*. Usually

written in loose iambic pentameter measures, the second line an incremental repeton of the first line, the third line a SYNTHETIC PARALLEL giving a consequence of the first two lines. Here is a schematic diagram of two blues stanzas:

lines	meters and rhymes	lines	meters and rhymes
1.	x́x x́x x́x x́x x́A	4.	x́x x́x x́x x́x x́B
2.	x́x x́x x́x x́x x́A	5.	x́x x́x x́x x́x x́B
3.	x́x x́x x́x x́x x́a	6.	x́x x́x x́x x́x x́b

Here is a BLUES SONNET, consisting of four triplets of blues stanza plus a HEROIC COUPLET:

Envoi in a Boneyard

Just let me drop this note into the dark,
Yes, let me drop this note into the dark—
I'll light it with a match and watch it spark.

I'll sail it into night with fire and flare,
Fly it into darkness, see it flare
And wink out in those shadows circling there.

I'll watch it take its place among the stars,
Among the minor planets and the stars.
I'll hum the blues, not much—a couple bars—

Until the spark has died to inky ash,
And words have flickered into smoken ash.
Then I'll have me a sip of sour mash,

And lean against this marker made of stone
That will not last as long as ink or bone.
                                        —WESLI COURT

BOB AND WHEEL

The bob and wheel is an English accentual-syllabic QUINTET STANZA sometimes found in association with accentual poems as a tail (*cauda*) on a stanza or as a strophe of ANGLO-SAXON PROSODY; specifically, in the anonymously written medieval epic *Gawain and the Green Knight*

The final line of the accentual stanza proper is usually an enjambed line that is continued by the BOB: a line of verse composed of one or two verse feet—sometimes of only one headless iamb. The bob itself can be an enjambed line that is continued and completed by the WHEEL: four lines, each of which consists of three verse feet.

The bob rhymes with lines two (2) and four (4) of the wheel; lines one (1) and three (3) of the wheel rhyme with each other. The following is the structure of the entire bob and wheel:

lines	meters and rhymes
1.	. . . xx x́a—*bob*
2.	x́x x́x x́b ⎤
3.	x́x x́x x́a ⎟
4.	x́x x́x x́b ⎬ —*wheel*
5.	x́x x́x x́a ⎦

Gawain and the Green Knight is too long to quote here, of course, but a good modern version is found in John Gardner's *The Complete Works of the Gawain Poet* (Chicago, 1965). In the poem below, quatrains of Anglo-Saxon prosody precede the bobs and wheels, which in this specific case are *burdens*—bobs and wheels are not usually refrains.

The Magi Carol

Sheep of the fold, fowls of the storm,
In chill the child, chaste in his manger—
The kings are coming to crown a King
And here are we, waiting to welcome

> them together:
> We wish you joy again—
> Gale, oak & heather,
> Mistletoe & pine—
> In any winter weather.

Bearing gold, gifts of myrrh,
Of frankincense—seed of thyme,
Vervain and thorn, horn at the gate—
The Magi move among the snows

> together:
> We wish you joy again—
> Gale, oak & heather,
> Mistletoe & pine—
> In any winter weather.

Reap the heart of the hoar oak
With a scythe of ore, open the gate
Of the golden bough, bend to dream
Before the stable, the stall of fortune

> all together:
> We wish you joy again—
> Gale, oak & heather,
> Mistletoe & pine—
> In any winter weather.
>   —WESLI COURT

BREF DOUBLE

French. Syllabic. Lines can be of any *single* length. Fourteen
lines arranged in three QUATRAIN stanzas and a concluding
COUPLET. There are only three rhymes in the poem, but not
every line is rhymed. The *a* rhyme appears twice somewhere
within the three quatrains and once in the couplet. The *b*
rhyme does likewise. The *c* rhyme ends each quatrain.

A possible scheme:

lines	rhymes	lines	rhymes
1.	a	9.	x—*no rhyme*
2.	x—*no rhyme*	10.	a
3.	b	11.	x—*no rhyme*
4.	c	12.	c
5.	x—*no rhyme*	13.	a
6.	b	14.	b
7.	x—*no rhyme*		
8	c		

This form is thought to be an ancestor of the SONNET. Actually, the bref double is a QUATORZAIN: any stanza or poem of fourteen lines *other* than a sonnet. Other quatorzains with set forms are the BLUES SONNET, the SICILIAN SONNET, the SONETTO RISPETTO, and the TERZA RIMA SONNET.

The example given here is also an example of ECHO VERSE:

Bref Double à L'Écho

Echo, speak—I expect no answers, though.	Though
I address rock out of a cage—from this	This
Stalk of flesh, begotten of earth and sun.	Son
What may one do who has no wish to blaze?	Blaze
Through burning blood there move pure Being's winds,	Winds
Mindless, augmenting Chance's forging blow.	Blow
These simple facts: Do they apply to all?	All
In the balance, is there nothing else that weighs?	Ways
High and low are baffled—not queen or nun	None
Knows why the womb leads to this maze. The May	May
Bee—it buzzes into heat, swarms to count	Count
Blossom and bloom for what, beyond mere daze?	Days
I ask you clear: Why are we? Do you know?	No
Why all our multitudes? What shall be won?	One

—WESLI COURT

BUCOLICS

A minor subgenre of the genre of poetry, the general form of bucolics is internal rather than external; that is, bucolics are intended to contrast simple modes with complex modes of life. The subject matter of bucolics specifically concerns the exaltation of the natural over the cultivated man and of the country and rural life over the life of the town and city. Bucolics are essentially romantic in content and viewpoint; however, they have had a place in the literature of the Western world from classic times to the present.

Although there is no set external form for the subgenre, several forms have been associated with it. A number of English-language bucolics have been written in HEROIC SESTET (*ababcc⁵*) and iambic tetrameter SEXTILLAS (*aabccb* or *ababcc*).

The PASTORAL or IDYL deals on the surface, with country ways, especially with the doings of shepherds or other rural people, but its allegorical level is concerned with more generally applicable topics. The ECLOGUE is a pastoral cast in the form of a dialogue or monologue spoken by country folk, and the PASTORAL ELEGY combines elegy and bucolics, as the name of the form indicates: Readily available examples are "Thanatopsis" by William Cullen Bryant and "Elegy Written in a Country Churchyard" by Thomas Gray.

The PASTORAL ODE, like the pastoral elegy, is a combination of the two forms, except that the ode is more specifically commemorative and the poem can be set in one of the ODE forms.

The French PASTOURELLE is a narrative poem, intended to be humorous, in which a knight (who narrates the story) takes advantage of a country wench, or in which the girl outwits the knight.

BURLESQUE—*see* SATIRICS.

BURNS STANZA—*see* STANDARD HABBIE.

BYR A THODDAID *(bir a thó-ddeyed)*
Welsh. Syllabic. This QUATRAIN STANZA combines a COUPLET consisting of eight syllables per line with another couplet consisting of ten syllables in the first line and six syllables in the second line. In the ten-syllable line, the *main rhyme* is found before the end of the line, and the syllables that follow the main rhyme in the ten-syllable line must be *linked* by means of alliteration, assonance, or *secondary rhyme* with the early syllables of the first part of the six-syllable line. In this quatrain, either couplet can follow the other. Note that in

this scheme, primary or main rhymes are in capital letters; alliteration, assonances, or secondary rhymes are indicated by means of small letters:

lines	syllables and rhymes	lines	syllables and rhymes
1.	x x x x x x x A	5.	x x x x x x D x e
2.	x x x x x x x A	6.	e x x x x D
3.	x x x x x x x B x c	7.	x x x x x x x F
4.	x c x x x B	8.	x x x x x x x F

The following poem ends in a couplet of CYHYDEDD FER:

Huntsong for a Small Son

Dinogad's coat is specked with spots—
I made it out of pelts of stoats.
Flingabout, fling! Flingabout, flingabout!
Eight times the song we'll sing.

When your daddy went to the hunt,
Shouldered his spear, his staff in hand,
He called to the hounds that were hale and fleet,
"Fido, fetch! Bowser, trail!"

He caught fish in his little boat
Like a dragon after a stoat.
When your daddy climbed up the craggy rock
He brought back boar, buck, stag,

A stippled gamehen from the hills
And a trout from Oak Fountain Falls.
At whatever your daddy cocks his spear,
There he strikes bear, lynx, fox.

This is no boast, this is no lie—
If it escapes then it can fly.

—ANONYMOUS

CACCIA—*see* LYRICS.

CALLIGRAMME—*see* SPATIALS.

CANCIONE

A Spanish term applied to any stanzaic poem written in heptasyllabic or hendecasyllabic lines whose stanza patterns are NONCE FORMS invented by the poet. See CANSO and CANZO within LYRICS and CANZONE.

CANSO—*see* LYRICS.

CANTICLE—*see* LITURGICS.

CANZO—*see* LYRICS.

CANZONE

An Italian form structured, like the PINDARIC ODE, in three movements. Each movement, however, is divided into three stanzas. The first two stanzas (*piedi*) in each movement are structurally alike; the third stanza in each movement (the *sirima* or *cauda*) is structurally different from the piedi, but the structures of both piedi and sirima are nonce forms. The poem often closes with a *commiato* or valediction. The meters are usually heptasyllabic or hendecasyllabic.

CAPITOLO

A satiric TERZA RIMA.

CAROL

French and English. Generally speaking, a carol is simply a "joyous hymn." It originally had a more-or-less set form that consisted of a two-line burden or TEXTE COUPLET, rhyming A^1A^2, and any number of QUATRAIN stanzas, rhyming *bbba*. The last lines of these stanzas rhymed with the burden, or they echoed or repeated one or the other of the burden lines. Usually the meter was short, trimeter or tetrameter, with no set verse foot. The whole burden might be repeated at intervals.

A possible scheme:

lines	meters, rhymes, refrains		lines	meters, rhymes, refrains
1.	x́x x́x x́x x́A¹	*texte*	7.	x́x x́x x́x xc
2.	x́x x́x x́x x́A²		8.	x́x x́x x́x xc
3.	x́x x́x x́x xb		9.	x́x x́x x́x xc
4.	x́x x́x x́x xb		10.	x́x x́x x́x xa or A¹ or A²
5.	x́x x́x x́x x́x b		11.	x́x x́x x́x x́A¹
6.	x́x x́x x́x x́a or A¹ or A²		12.	x́x x́x x́x x́A²

For other forms that use a texte, see the GLOSE, the RONDEAU REDOUBLED and the SONNET REDOUBLED.

The Shepherds' Carol

Terly terlow, terly terlow,
Merry the shepherds began to blow!

About the field they piped full right,
Even about the midst of the night,
And down from heaven there came a light,
   Terly terlow, terly terlow!

Of angels there came a company
With merry songs and melody;
The shepherds anon did them espy—
   Merry the shepherds began to blow!

"Gloria in excelsis!" the angels sung
And said that peace was present among
All men that to the faith had clung,
   Terly terlow, terly terlow!

The shepherds hied them to Bethlehem
To see that blessed sun abeam,
And there they found that glorious stream—
   Merry the shepherds began to blow!

Now pray we to that meekest child
And to his mother that is so mild
Who shall be forever undefiled,
   Terly terlow, terly terlow!

Terly terlow, terly terlow,
Merry the shepherds began to blow!
                —ANONYMOUS

In the following poem, Wyatt used the carol stanza not to gloss a texte but to gloss the first phrase of the first line, which became the refrain:

What Meaneth This?

What meaneth this? When I lie alone
I toss, I turn, I sigh, I groan:
My bed meseems as hard as stone.
   What meaneth this?

I sigh, I plain continually:
The clothes that on my bed do lie,
Always methink they lie awry.
   What meaneth this?

In slumbers oft for fear I quake;
For heat and cold I burn and shake;
For lack of sleep my head doth ache.
   What meaneth this?

And if perchance by me there pass
She unto whom I sue for grace,
The cold blood forsaketh my face.
   What meaneth this?

But if I sit to her nearby,
With a loud voice my heart doth cry,
And yet my mouth is dumb and dry.
   What meaneth this?

To ask for help no heart I have;
My tongue doth fail what I should crave;
Yet inwardly I rage and rave.
   What meaneth this?

Thus have I passed many a year
And many a day, though naught appear
But most of that which most I fear.
   What meaneth this?
      —THOMAS WYATT

For other forms that gloss the poem's initial phrase, see the RONDEAU and the ROUNDEL. For another example of the carol, see "The Magi Carol" in the section on the BOB AND WHEEL and "The Wind Carol" in *Strong Measures* (op. cit.).

CASBAIRDNE *(coss-búyer-dne)*

Irish. Syllabic. A QUATRAIN stanza of heptasyllabic lines with trisyllabic endings. Lines two (2) and four (4) rhyme, and lines one (1) and three (3) consonate with them. There are at least two cross-rhymes in each couplet. In the *first* couplet, these cross-rhymes need not be exact. There is alliteration as in RANNAIGHEACHT MHOR, the final syllable of line four (4) alliterating with *the preceding stressed word*.

   The *poem* (not the stanza) ends with the same first syllable, word, or line with which it begins. A simplified scheme:

lines   *syllables and rhymes*

1.   x *x b x* (x x ac) ⎫
                      ⎬ —*consonate*
2.   x *a x x* (x x bc) ⎭

3.   x *x x b* (x x dc) ⎫
                      ⎬ —*consonate*
4.   x *x c x* (x x bc) ⎭

The poem that follows is modified casbairdne—the trisyllabic line endings have not been adhered to:

The Ruin

Well wrought, this wall that Weird felled.
The fort failed, smoke cast its pall,
Snapped tall rooves: towers fallen
On the trollmen's stone-hard hall.

Rime scoiled gatekeeps; the mortar
Shattered, slate showershields moulder.
Age ate them, wright and wielder;
Earthgrip clasps builder, elder

And son, in gravegrasp lichen.
Kings fell often under stone
And storm, first slain by weapon:
Arch crashed, stricken, on bare bone.

To soilcrust sank works of skill:
A mood-quick skull bound the wall
All in iron—what wit and will!
Cunning wonders, well-fixed, fall.

Among these hearths ran hot springs;
In horngabled wings rang throngs;
Men filled meadhalls, long buildings.
Weird made silence of strong song.

There came days of death and pest;
The folk were lost, their flower snatched.
Where they fought, vetch carpets waste,
Ruins where they faced the Fetch.

Henchmen who would build are cinched
In loamclench under this arch
Breeched and broken, wried and wrenched
Groundward from the roof-ridge reach.

There once many a mood-glad wight,
Garnished gold-bright, in wine-pride,
Gazed wide on gems, silver wrought
And fought for from tide to tide;

On wealth held, bared in a hoard
Where hoar now holds the brave, broad
Burg, here where the goodman stood
In amber hearing loud laud.

Homes were sealed, the ring-tank walled
Till time failed it, with it melled,
Stopped streams where they snelled and coiled,
Boiled to the baths till Weird welled.

—ANONYMOUS

CATALOG POEM

The catalog is a listing of parts of speech in parallel structures. Christopher Smart's "Of the Spiritual Musick," previously quoted, is an example. See also PROSE POEM.

CATCH—*see* CACCIA, LYRICS, ROUNDELAY.

CENTO

A pastiche poem compiled from the works or notebooks of a dead poet. Here is a cento in quantitative syllabic verse from the letters of Emily Dickinson:

Poetry

Memory's fog is rising: I had a terror
   I could tell to none—and so I sing,
    as the boy does in the burying ground,
because I am afraid. When a sudden light
on the orchards, or a new fashion in the wind

troubled my attention, I felt a palsy,
   here, the verses just relieve.
                  I am
   small, like the wren, and my hair is bold,
like the chestnut burr, and my eyes like sherry
in the glass the guest leaves. There is always one

thing to be grateful for—that one is one's self
   and not somebody else. "We thank thee,
    oh loving Father," for these strange minds
that enamor us against Thee.
                  If I read
a book, and it makes my body so cold no

fire can ever warm me, I know *that* is
   poetry. If I feel physically
    as if the top of my head were
taken off, I know *that* is poetry. These are
the only ways I know it. Is there any

other way?
            How does the poet learn to grow,
    or is it unconveyed, like witchcraft
    or melody? I had no monarch
in my life and cannot rule myself. When I
try to organize, my little force explodes,

leaves me bare and charred. I marked a line in one
    verse, because I met it after I
    made it and never consciously touch
a paint mixed by another person. I do
not let go of it, because it is mine.

Two editors of journals came and asked me
    for my mind. When I asked them, "Why?" they
    said I was penurious—they'd use it
for the world. I could not weigh my self myself—
my size felt small to me. One hears of Mister

Whitman—I never read his book, but was told
    he is disgraceful. To my thought, "To
    publish" is foreign as firmament
to fin. My barefoot rank is better. If fame
belonged to me, I could not escape her—if

she did not, the longest day would pass me on
    the chase.
            There seems a spectral power
    in thought that walks alone. I find
ecstasy in living—the mere sense of life
is joy enough. The chestnut hit my notice

suddenly, and I thought the skies in blossom!

CHANSO

A French form, syllabic and rhymed. Lines can be of any
single length. It contains five or six identically structured
stanzas, plus an envoi that mirrors the structure of the last
half of the stanza pattern. Although the stanza pattern and
rhyme scheme are rigid, the form is a nonce form set by
the poet.

CHANSON DE GESTE—*see* NARRATIVES.
CHANT—*see* CHANT ROYAL *and* LYRICS.

CHANTE-FABLE
A medieval French romance written in alternating verse and prose passages.

CHANTEY—*see* LYRICS.

CHANT ROYAL
A French form. Syllabic. Lines can be of any single length, but are usually either octosyllabic or decasyllabic or, in accentual-syllabics, iambic tetrameter or pentameter. There are sixty lines divided into five, eleven-line stanzas and one, five-line envoy. The chant royal turns on five rhymes and is built on a refrain. Strictly speaking, it is a form of the BALLADE.

This scheme shows the structure of all stanzas:

lines	rhymes
1.	a
2.	b
3.	a
4.	b
5.	c
6.	c
7.	d
8.	d
9.	e
10.	d
11.	E—*refrain*

This is the scheme of the envoy:

56.	d
57.	d
58.	e
59.	d
60.	E—*refrain*

For a contemporary example that uses consonance rather than true rhyme, see Robert Morgan's "Chant Royal" in *Strong Measures* (op. cit.).

CHARMS—*see* ANAGRAM *and* LYRICS.

CHAUCERIAN STANZA—*see* RIME ROYAL.

CHOKA

The choka is a Japanese form. It can be of any length, as long as it is written in alternating five- and seven-syllable lines and ends with a seven-syllable line. It is unrhymed. For an example, see "Paradigm" in the section on the KATAUTA among FORENSICS. For forms related to the choka, see the MONDO, KATAUTA, SEDOKA, TANKA, SOMONKA, RENGA, and HAIKU.

CHORAL ODE—*see* ODE.

CHORIAMBICS

Greek. Accentual-syllabic. A *line* consisting of, in this order, two trochees, an iamb, a trochee, an iamb, a trochee, and two iambs. Unrhymed. Poems can consist of any number of lines. The scheme for one line:

line　　　　*meters*

1.　　xx xx xx xx xx xx xx xx

　Coming down the decayed stairs he began falling between the slats.

CINQUAIN

An American form. Syllabic or accentual-syllabic. Five lines long, the lines consist of two, four, six, eight, and two syllables, respectively. It is unrhymed, and a set form of the QUINTET. Originally the poem was written in iambs: one iambic foot in the first line, two in the second, three in the third, four in the fourth, and one in the fifth.

Here is the scheme in syllabics:

lines	syllables
1.	x x
2.	x x x x
3.	x x x x x x
4.	x x x x x x x x
5.	x x

The following is an ancient Irish poem cast in the form of a cinquain—note that it fulfills the bardic requirement that it end with the same word it begins with:

Evil It Is

Evil
It is to shun
The king of righteousness
And to make a compact with the
Devil.

—ANONYMOUS

CLASSICAL HEXAMETER—*see* HEXAMETER.

CLASSICAL PENTAMETER—*see* PENTAMETER.

CLERIHEW

A quatrain epigram in dipodic rhythms, rhyming *aabb,* the first line of which is the name of a person. The three following lines give a "capsule biography" that lampoons the person named.

CLOGYRNACH *(clog-ír-nach)*

A Welsh form. Syllabic. A SESTET STANZA having lines with counts of eight, eight, five, five, three, and three syllables, respectively (8−8−5−5−3−3). The two, three-syllable lines may, if desired, be written as one, six-syllable line. The rhyme scheme is *aabbba.*

A diagram of one stanza of clogyrnach follows:

lines	syllables and rhymes
1.	x x x x x x x a
2.	x x x x x x x a
3.	x x x x x b
4.	x x x x x b
5.	x x b
6.	x x a

In Summer

Summer I love, stallions abroad,
Knights courageous before their lord;
    The comber booming,
    Apple tree blooming,
  Shield shining, war-shouldered.

Longing, I went craving, alack—
The bowing of the slim hemlock,
    In bright noon, dawn's sleight;
    Fair frail form smooth, white,
  Her step light on the stalk.

Silent is the small deer's footfall,
Scarcely older than she is tall.
    Comely, beautiful,
    Bred bountiful,
  Passion will heed her call,

But no vile word will pass her lips.
I pace, I plead—when shall we tryst?
    When will you meet me?
    Love drowns me deeply—
  Christ keep me! He knows best.
    —HYWEL AB OWAIN GWYNEDD

COBLA

A French term for a poem of one stanza.

COMMIATO—*see* CANZONE.

COMMON MEASURE

Accentual-syllabic. Rhymed. A QUATRAIN STANZA written in iambics, unlike the podic BALLAD STANZA, which is otherwise similar. The rhyme scheme is *abcb*. The first and third lines consist of four iambic feet; the second and fourth lines, of three iambic feet. A simple scheme of the stanza would thus be $a^4b^3c^4b^3$. A complete scheme would be:

lines	meters and rhymes
1.	x x́ x x́ x x́ x á
2.	x x́ x x́ x b́
3.	x x́ x x́ x x́ x ć
4.	x x́ x x́ x b́

For an example, see Robert Burns' "A Red, Red Rose" on p. 34. HYMNAL STANZA is the same, except that it rhymes *abab*.

SHORT MEASURE, a form of common measure, rhymes and meters $a^3b^3c^4b^3$. SHORT HYMNAL STANZA is similar, $a^3b^3a^4b^3$:

The Elixir

> Teach me, my God and King,
> In all things thee to see,
> And what I do in any thing,
> To do it as for thee:
>
> Not rudely, as a beast,
> To run into an action;
> But still to make thee prepossessed
> And give it his perfection.
>
> A man that looks on glass,
> On it may stay his eye;
> Or if he pleaseth, through it pass
> And then the heaven espy.
>
> All may of thee partake:
> Nothing can be so mean,

Which with his tincture (for thy sake)
   Will not grow bright and clean.

   A servant with this clause
   Makes drudgery divine:
Who sweeps a room, as for thy laws,
   Makes that and the action fine.

   This is the famous stone
   That turneth all to gold:
For that which God doth touch and own
   Cannot for less be sold.

           —GEORGE HERBERT

LONG MEASURE rhymes *abcb,* but all lines are iambic tetrameter, as are the lines in LONG HYMNAL STANZA, which rhymes *abab:*

The Mourning of the Hare

By a forest I began to fare,
Walking by myself alone,
When I heard the mourning of a hare—
Ruefully she made her moan:

"Dear worthy God, how shall I be living
And lead my life upon the land?
From dale to down am I driven;
Nowhere may I sit or stand!

"I may neither rest nor sleep
By any wallway ever so tall,
Nor no covert may me keep,
But ever I run from hole to hole.

"Hunters will not be remiss
In hope of hunting for to wend.
They leash their hounds more or less
And bring them to the far field's end;

"Anon, as they come up behind,
I look and sit full still and low;
That man who is the first to find
Me cries aloud, 'Ho! Tally-ho!'

"All winter in the deepest snow
Men seek about to find my trace,
And by my footprints I am known—
They follow me from place to place,

"And if I sit and crop the cale
Whenas the wife be in the way,
Shortly she swears, 'By the cock's soul,
There is a hare within my hay!'

"Ere ever I may start to flee,
The greyhounds run me to the grave;
My bowels they be thrown away,
And I am borne home on a stave."
                    —ANONYMOUS

All forms of common measure and hymnal stanza can be doubled to make OCTAVE STANZAS. These forms are called, respectively, COMMON OCTAVE, HYMNAL OCTAVE, SHORT OCTAVE, SHORT HYMNAL OCTAVE, LONG OCTAVE, and LONG HYMNAL OCTAVE. For an example of hymnal octave, see "Robin and Makyn" in the section on the ECLOGUE DEBAT.

SHORT PARTICULAR MEASURE is a SESTET STANZA that has three iambic feet in lines one, two, four, and five, and four feet in lines three and six. It usually rhymes $a^3a^3b^4a^3a^3b^4$. For a reversal of this pattern, see RIME COUÉE. This poem is a variation of short particular measure:

A Song Out of the Italian

To thy lover,
    Dear, discover
That sweet blush of thine that shameth
    (When those roses
    It discloses)
All the flowers that Nature nameth.

In free air
    Flow thy hair
That no more summer's best dresses
    Be beholden

For their golden
Locks to Phoebus' flaming tresses.

O deliver
Love his quiver,
From thy eyes he shoots his arrows
Where Apollo
Cannot follow,
Feathered with his mother's sparrows.

O envy not
(That we dye not)
Those dear lips whose door encloses
All the graces
In their places,
Brother pearls and sister roses.

From these treasures
Of ripe pleasures
One bright smile to clear the weather.
Earth and Heaven
Thus made even,
Both will be good friends together.

The air does woo thee,
Winds cling to thee,
Might a word once fly from out thee;
Storm and thunder
Would sit under,
And keep silence round about thee.

But if Nature's
Common creatures
So dear glories dare not borrow,
Yet thy beauty
Owes a duty
To my loving, lingering sorrow.

When to end me
Death shall send me
All his terrors to affright me;
Thine eyes' graces

> Gild their faces,
> And those terrors shall delight me!
>
> When my dying
> Life is flying,
> Those sweet airs that often slew me
> Shall revive me
> Or reprieve me,
> And to many deaths renew me.
> —RICHARD CRASHAW

Strong Measures (op. cit.) contains many examples of contemporary poems written in the common measure forms.

COMPLAINT

A verse monologue that complains of the state of the poet, of an unrequited love or of a more trivial situation, and that begs for easement. For a modern form of the complaint, see the BLUES STANZA.

CORONACH—*see* DIRGE *under* LYRICS.

COUPLET

Any two lines, written as a unit. A couplet can be any length and in any meter. Most couplets rhyme *aa,* but this rhyme scheme is not a requirement. There are several set forms.

The SHORT COUPLET is written in either iambic or trochaic tetrameter. The pattern in iambics looks like this:

lines	meters and rhymes
1.	xx xx xx xa
2.	xx xx xx xa

The SPLIT COUPLET is also accentual-syllabic. It consists of two lines, the first written in iambic pentameter measure, the second, in iambic dimeter:

1.	xx xx xx xx xa
2.	xx xa

Lafe Grat
(*from* Bordello)

In this house I am not ugly—nowhere
else. Nor is there
a mirror in the room we use, my bought
bride and I. What
Images are reflected in her eyes
I recognize
as in a dream only, my face redrawn
by night. Reborn
each evening of this woman, spared my name,
the cruel fame
of the publicly disfigured, I roar
with my old whore
like a whole man, transfigured for a time.
Sordid? I am
Lafe Grat. I work hard to make a living.
There's no giving
to a man who makes you think of darkness,
for my likeness
is found buried in everyone, hidden
till, unbidden,
it rises to gorge the beast in the blood.
So, out of mud
I am formed and rise each morning to stalk
where others walk
in a world of surfaces—till night when,
like other men,
I may purchase with coin my manhood, life—
a moment's wife.

—L. T.

The following poem is written in SESTET NONCE STANZAS.
The first four lines are two split couplets, the last two lines of
each stanza form a HEROIC COUPLET:

On a Sea-Storm Nigh the Coast

All round the horizon black clouds appear;
                    a storm is near:

Darkness eclipseth the serener sky,
        The winds are high,
Making the surface of the Ocean show
Like mountains lofty, and like valleys low.

The weighty seas are rowled from the deeps
        In mighty heaps,
And from the rocks' foundations do arise
        To kiss the skies.
Wave after wave in hills each other crowds,
As if the deeps resolved to storm the clouds.

How did the surging billows foam and roar
        Against the shore
Threatening to bring the land under their power
        And it devour:
Those liquid mountains on the cliffs were hurled
As to a chaos they would shake the world.

The Earth did interpose the Prince of Light,
        'Twas sable night:
All darkness was but when the lightnings fly
        And light the sky,
Night, thunder, lightning, rain, and *raging* wind,
To make a storm had all their forces joined.
              —RICHARD STEERE

An ALEXANDRINE COUPLET is made of two rhyming ALEX-ANDRINE LINES and is often used as a coda, as in the heroic couplets above.

The QASIDA, an Arabic form, consists of any number of couplets, up to one hundred, all turning on the same rhyme:

Delight in Books from Evening

Delight in books from evening
Till midnight when the cocks do sing,
Till morning when the day doth spring:
Till sunset when the bell doth ring.
Delight in books, for books do bring
Poor men to learn most every thing;
The art of true leveling:

Yea, even how to please the king.
Delight in books, they're carrying
Us so far, that we know to fling
On waspish men (who, taking wing,
Surround us) that they can not sting.
              —FRANCIS DANIEL PASTORIUS

For another example of the qasida, see Robert Herrick's "Anacrontick Verse" under ANACREONTICS in the section on LYRICS.

There are three Welsh couplets, all of them syllabic. CYHY-DEDD FER (cuh-hée-dedd ver) is a rhymed couplet, each line containing eight syllables; for an example, see the last couplet of "Huntsong for a Small Son" in BYR A THODDAID.

Each line of the CYWYDD DEUAIR FYRION (ców-idd dyé-ire vúhr-yon) contains four syllables, and it is rhymed:

My Choice

I choose a fair
Maid so slender
Tall and silver,
Her gown of heather
Hue—I choose her,
Nature's daughter,
For the kind word
Dropped, scarcely heard,
And for my part
Take her to heart
For gift, for grace,
For her embrace.

I choose the wave,
The water's shade;
Witch of the shire,
Your Welsh tongue pure,
My choice you are,
And am I yours?
Why be silent?
(Sweet your silence!)

I choose my course
Without remorse,
With a clear voice—
So clear a choice.
  —HYWEL AB OWAIN GWYNEDD

CYWYDD DEUAIR HIRION (ców-idd dyé-ire heer-yon) is a light-rhyming, seven-syllable couplet—that is, the first line is masculine (ending on a stressed syllable) and the second line is feminine (ending on an unstressed syllable). Because of this stress requirement, the prosody of this form is properly not syllabics but syllabic-accentuals, as distinguished from accentual-syllabics. The lines rhyme *aa*. A possible schematic diagram for two couplets (note that the stress pattern, except for the light rhymes, is not regular) would be:

lines	syllables, rhymes, stresses	lines	syllables, rhymes, stresses
1.	x́ x́ x́ x x́ x a	3.	x́ x x́ x́ x x b
2.	x x́ x x x́ x a	4.	x x x́ x x x b

Lament for Owain Ab Urien

Owain ab Urien's soul
May the Lord keep immortal.
Lordly to praise Rheged's lord,
Greatly burdened by greensward,
Laid low, this far-bruited king,
His lances wings of dawning.
To none other was he thrall,
No other was his equal,
Reaper of foes, ravener,
Son, father, and grandfather.
When Owain scythed down Fflamddwyn
It was no more than nodding.
Sleeping are the Anglemen,
Light in their sockets open,
And those who but shortly fled
Were bolder than they needed—

Owain put them to the sack:
Sheep before the wolf-pack.
Grand in colored armament,
Well he horsed the suppliant:
For his soul's sake Owain shared
The treasure that he hoarded.
Owain ab Urien's soul
May the Lord keep immortal.
                              —TALIESIN

For other set forms of the couplet, see the sections on DI-
DACTICS, HEROICS, and POULTER'S MEASURE. See also the LA-
MENT in the section on LYRICS. Synonyms for couplet are
DISTICH and TWIME.

CYHYDEDD FER—*see* COUPLET.

CYHYDEDD HIR *(cuh-hée-dedd heer)*
Welsh. Syllabic. OCTAVE STANZAS composed of two QUA-
TRAINS, each of whose four lines consist of five, five, five,
and four (5–5–5–4) syllables, respectively. Each quatrain
may, if desired, be arranged as a single, nineteen-syllable
line. The five-syllable lines in each quatrain rhyme with one
another; the four-syllable lines carry the main rhyme.
    Strictly speaking, the stanzas need not be octave stanzas.
Any number of quatrains can be used in a stanza and, tech-
nically, the meter will remain cyhydedd hir. However, within
any stanza the short lines must carry the same rhyme.
    The scheme of two octave stanzas would be:

lines	syllables and rhymes	lines	syllables and rhymes
1.	x x x x a	9.	x x x x d
2.	x x x x a	10.	x x x x d
3.	x x x x a	11.	x x x x d
4.	x x x B	12.	x x x E
5.	x x x x c	13.	x x x x f
6.	x x x x c	14.	x x x x f
7.	x x x x c	15.	x x x x f
8.	x x x B	16.	x x x E

To a Girl

I saw on the face
Of a haughty lass
A look with no trace
    Of love—cold, still:
The cresting spume-glow
Upon the billow
Of the sea's face, flow
    And ebb of chill.

She sends her respects
To me, harshly, vexed—
The candle rejects,
    Cuts shadow dead,
And now I must hoard
Disgrace's great hurt—
She's trod on my heart,
    Sought Greeneye's bed!
        —CYNDDELW BRYDYDD MAWR

CYHYDEDD NAW BAN *(cuh-hée-dedd naw ban)*
Welsh. Syllabic. A *line* of nine syllables. It *must* rhyme with
at least one other line of equal length to form a couplet. It
can continue the rhyme throughout the stanza, which can be
of any length, provided that all lines are equal in length.

The scheme for two lines is:

lines   syllables and rhymes
  1.   x x x x x x x x a
  2.   x x x x x x x x a

This form should not be confused with the QASIDA. The fol-
lowing example is an excerpt, the first stanza only of a much
longer poem:

In Praise of Owain Gwynedd

I hail a boonsman hearty in war,
Battlewolf, boastful, first to the fore—
I sing of serving him with fervor,

Sing his mead-fed and worthy power,
Sing his ardor, this wind-winged falcon,
Sing his thoughts, lofty as the welkin,
Sing his dauntless deeds, lord of frayhounds,
Sing his praises—they may know no bounds,
Sing odes for my magnanimous thane;
I sing paeans of praise for Owain.
                —CYNDDELW BRYDYDD MAWR

CYRCH A CHWTA *(kirch a chóo-tah)*

Welsh. Syllabic. An OCTAVE STANZA of six rhyming or con-
sonating, seven-syllable lines plus a couplet, the *second* line
of which rhymes with the first six lines. The first line of the
couplet, line seven (7), cross-rhymes into the third, fourth,
or fifth syllable of line eight (8). The scheme for one stanza is:

lines	syllables and rhymes
1.	x x x x x x a
2.	x x x x x x a
3.	x x x x x x a
4.	x x x x x x a
5.	x x x x x x a
6.	x x x x x x a
7.	x x x x x x b
8.	x x *x* b x x a

CYWYDD DEUAIR FYRION—*see* COUPLET.

CYWYDD DEUAIR HIRION—*see* COUPLET.

CYWYDD LLOSGYRNOG *(ców-idd llos-gír-nog)*

A Welsh form. Syllabic. A SESTET STANZA, the lines having
respective syllable counts of eight, eight, seven, eight, eight,
and seven (8–8–7–8–8–7). Lines one (1) and two (2) rhyme
and cross-rhyme with the *middle* syllable of line three (3);
lines four (4) and five (5) rhyme and cross-rhyme with the
middle syllable of line six (6); lines three (3) and six (6)
rhyme with each other. This form should not be confused

with RIME COUÉE, which has a similar rhyme scheme. Here is
the schematic for a stanza:

lines	syllables and rhymes
1.	x x x x x x x a
2.	x x x x x x x a
3.	x x x a x x b
4.	x x x x x x x c
5.	x x x x x x x c
6.	x x x c x x b

The Rule of Three

When I consider these things three
I may never then go blithely:
I shall, firstly, wend away;
Secondly, I know not the hour.
The third fills me with my most fear—
I know not where I shall stray.
—ANONYMOUS

DEACHNADH MOR—*see* RANNAIGHEACHTS.

DEBAT, DEBATE—*see* FORENSICS.

DECASTICH
Any ten-line poem.

DEIBHIDHE *(jay-vée)*
Irish. Syllabic-accentual. A QUATRAIN STANZA light-rhyming
in couplets. There is alliteration between two words in
each line, the final word of line four (4) alliterating with the
preceding stressed word. There are at least two cross-rhymes
between lines three (3) and four (4). Each line has seven
syllables.

The poem (not the stanza) ends with the same first syl-
lable, word, or line with which it begins (the poem given
here as an example does not observe this convention). The
diagram for one stanza:

lines	*syllables, rhymes, stressed endings*
1.	x x x x x x́ a
2.	x x x x x x́ a
3.	x b x x x x b́
4.	x x x b x x́ b

The Death of Conain

The shining tides rise and swell,
Swing him in his coracle,
Break across the sandy strand:
Conain looks out at the land,

Then she whose white hair he grips—
Hair of spindrift, frigid lips—
Fleers and turns her phlegm to foam
On the tomb that was his home.
　　　　　—ANONYMOUS

DESCORT

A French form whose only requirement is that each line of the poem be different from every other line in all ways (discordant). The descort mixes meters, line-lengths, and stanza lengths and is itself of no fixed length.

DIDACTICS

Didactics is a minor subgenre of the literary genre called poetry. Didactic poetry is instructional (teaching poetry); its purpose is to give instructions or information regarding some subject. There are traditionally four didactic forms in English literature.

The EPISTLE is a loose form, a letter to someone in particular or to mankind in general:

An Epistle to Two Friends
To Dr. Helsham

Nov. 23, at night, 1731.

Sir,
When I left you, I found myself of the grape's juice sick;
I'm so full of pity I never abuse sick;
And the patientest patient ever you knew sick;
Both when I am purge-sick, and when I am spew-sick.
I pitied my cat, whom I knew by her mew sick:
She mended at first, but now she's anew sick.
Captain Butler made some in the church black and blue sick.
Dean Cross, had he preached, would have made us all pew-
    sick.
Are not you, in a crowd when you sweat and you stew, sick?
Lady Santry got out of the church when she grew sick,
And as fast as she could, to the deanery flew sick.
Miss Morice was (I can assure you 'tis true) sick:
For, who would not be in that numerous crew sick?
Such music would make a fanatic or Jew sick,
Yet, ladies are seldom at ombre or loo sick.
Nor is old Nanny Shales, whene'er she does brew, sick.
My footman came home from the church of a bruise sick,
And looked like a rake, who was made in the stews sick:
But you learned doctors can make whom you choose sick:
And poor I myself was, when I withdrew, sick:
For the smell of them made me like garlic and rue sick,
And I got through the crowd, though not led by a clew, sick.
Yet hoped to find many (for that was your cue) sick;
But there was not a dozen (to give them their due) sick,
And those, to be sure, stuck together like glue sick.
So are ladies in crowds, when they squeeze and they screw, sick;
You may find they are all, by their yellow pale hue, sick;
So am I, when tobacco, like Robin, I chew, sick.

To Dr. Sheridan

Nov. 23, at night.

If I write any more, it will make my poor Muse sick.
This night I came home with a very cold dew sick,

And I wish I may soon be not of an ague sick;
But I hope I shall ne'er be like you, of a shrew sick,
Who often has made me, by looking askew, sick.
                              —JONATHAN SWIFT

The PRIMER COUPLET, a set form, is a dipodic couplet,
rhyming *aa*. Usually, primer couplets are rhymed aphorisms:

Obadiah

Obadiah
Jumped in the fire,
Fire was hot,
He jumped in the pot,
The pot was so little
He jumped in the kettle,
The kettle was so black
He jumped in the crack,
The crack was so high
He jumped in the sky,
The sky was so blue
He jumped in the canoe,
The canoe was so deep
He jumped in the creek,
The creek was so shallow
He jumped in the tallow,
The tallow was so hard
He jumped in the lard,
The lard was so soft
He jumped in the loft,
The loft was so rotten
He fell in the cotton,
The cotton so warm
He stayed till the morn.
                              —ANONYMOUS

The RIDDLE is a short lyric that poses a question, the an-
swer to which lies hidden in hints:

Three Riddles from the Anglo-Saxon

i.
The world's wonder,
                    I liven wenches,
A boon to townsfolk,
                    a bane to none,
Though haply I prick
                    her who picks me.
Well planted,
                    I stand in a bed
With my rogue root.
                        Rarely, mayhap,
Some carline,
                    careless and daring,
Rasps my red tip,
                        wrenches my head,
Lays me to larder.
                        I teach her lore,
This curly-hair
                    who clasps me thus,
And after our meeting
                        moisten her eye.

ii.
Fire-fretted,
                    I flirt with wind;
Limbs light-fraught,
                            I strive to fly:
A grove of leaves,
                    a glowing flinder.
Hand to hand,
                    I ring the hall—
Lords and ladies
                    love to toast me.
When I heighten
                    and all the folk
Bow before me,
                    then their blessings
Shall soar beneath
                    my befriending gloaming.

iii.
Swung at thigh,
           a wizard thing!
Below his belt,
           beneath the folds
Of robes I dangle
           with my single eye.
Stiff and stout,
           I swivel about.
Aiming the head
           of his well-hung tool,
My holder hoists
           his hem knee-high:
He wants to fill
           a famous hole
That I fit well
           at length and more—
What will be filled
           has been filled before.
           —ANONYMOUS

Answers: (i) an onion; (ii) a wooden torch; (iii) a key.

GEORGICS are rhymed instructions or directions in the arts, sciences, or trades—versified handbooks. An excellent modern georgic is David Wagoner's "Staying Alive," widely anthologized and included in *Poetry: An Introduction* (op. cit.). See also BESTIARY for another didactic form.

The *classical discourse* is a model structure for expository writing:

A. *Subject*. The subject of the discourse is given in the title.
B. *Thesis*. The *exordium* is the statement of the subject being examined and an introduction to the author's thesis. It differs from the subject in that it is a *complete statement*, usually given in one independent clause or sentence.
C. *Argument*.
    1. The *narratio* is the exposition of necessary background information concerning subject and thesis.

2. The *confirmatio* is the list of arguments, proofs, and facts backing the thesis. It is usually arranged in the order of weakest argument to strongest (climactic).

3. The *refutatio* is the rebuttal of all possible arguments to the contrary. It is usually arranged in the order of strongest argument to weakest (anticlimactic).

D. *Conclusion.* The *peroratio* is an appeal to emotion as well as to logic, the restatement of the proved thesis, and the conclusion of the discourse.

The poem "The Old Professor," in *Poetry: An Introduction* (op. cit.), is a classical discourse. Alexander Pope's *Essay on Criticism* is a pertinent verse essay as well, but too long to quote here. It is, however, easily available. Some didactic techniques commonly found in the classical discourse and in other arguments follow:

Apophasis is the rhetorical technique of denying your intention to speak about a particular point, at the same time, mentioning it— "I don't intend to mention the fact that Mr. Jones was convicted for larceny."

Metastasis is the technique of flitting quickly from one argument to another, much as a boxer bobs and weaves so that his opponent cannot get a good shot at him.

Paragon is the argumentative technique of quickly summing up and rejecting all reasons for making a particular point, except the one reason the arguer believes to be valid.

Parecnasis is the technique of digression, leaving the main argument for a time to talk of other things that, for the moment, may not seem pertinent, but that, in fact, bolster the main point when it is returned to.

Stasis is the technique of dwelling at length upon one's strongest argument.

Many didactic poems, however, do not argue, they harangue—notice that lyricism is often used to "carry" the message of the poem, and that when the sonic level is not emphasized (not to mention the ideational level), the sensory level is.

DIMINISHING VERSE—*see* ECHO VERSE.

DIRGE—*see* CORONACH, MONODY, THRENODY.

DISTICH—*see* COUPLET.

DIT—*see* EXEMPLUM.

DITHYRAMB—*see* LYRICS.

DITTY—*see* LYRICS.

DIZAIN—*see* BALLADE.

DOUBLE ACROSTIC—*see* ACROSTIC.

DOUBLE BALLADE—*see* BALLADE.

DOUBLE BALLADE SUPREME—*see* BALLADE.

DRAMATIC MONOLOGUE—*see* DRAMATICS.

DRAMATICS

A major subgenre of poetry, dramatic works are written to be spoken aloud. There are several stage forms:

TRAGEDY is a form of verse drama in which a heroic protagonist struggles to avoid his or her inevitable defeat (fate). Its elements are the balance of pathos and terror as the protagonist courageously faces the human predicament; the paradox of nobility of character combined with human fallibility; theatrical narration by means of concrete, mimetic stage actions; masked or stylized characters who are representative not of abstractions as such but, first, of historical or mythological figures and, second, of types of people; two choruses, usually representative of Everyman, that comment on the action; and a set, formal structure consisting of speeches, odes, choral odes, and stylized stage actions of various kinds. An example of a modern tragedy is T. S. Eliot's *Murder in the Cathedral*.

COMEDY is tragedy burlesqued. The protagonist is a humorous, not an empathetic, character, and the stages leading to his/her defeat or, possibly, triumph are humorous as well.

TRAGICOMEDY is a verse or a compound-mode drama. It combines tragedy and comedy, usually in a plot-subplot relationship. Good is rewarded and vice punished.

The MASK is a relatively short verse or compound-mode drama performed by masked figures. It includes songs, speeches, dances, mimes, and spectacle. It was a forerunner of opera. Current masks are largely literary rather than dramatic—e. e. cummings wrote masks, among them one called *Santa Claus,* and Frost wrote some as well, including *A Masque of Mercy.*

The MORALITY PLAY is a verse or compound-mode allegory in the form of a play. It rehearses the pilgrimage of man's progress toward death and his hope of salvation from sin through repentance and submission to God's mercy. Other than the pilgrimage, the elements are the *psychomachia,* or the strife of the Seven Deadly Sins aided by the Vices with the Four Cardinal and Three Theological Virtues over possession of Everyman's soul, and the *totentanz* or Dance of Death. Other personified abstractions are Conscience, Conviction of Sin, and Repentance.

The MYSTERY PLAY is based upon the Biblical story of man's Creation, Fall, and Redemption; the MIRACLE PLAY is concerned with the life and martyrdom of a saint; and the PASSION PLAY deals with the events in the life of Christ before the Resurrection—between the Last Supper and the Crucifixion.

The NOH PLAY is a Japanese compound-mode drama, somewhat similar to the mask and to tragedy. It is allusive and impressionistic. It uses traditional subjects, masked figures, a chorus, mime, dance, music, and choreographed movement. William Butler Yeats wrote modern plays that were influenced by the noh.

Most poets today, however, write primarily for the page, and there are three general forms outside drama proper:

A DIALOGUE is a conversation among two or more characters.

A MONOLOGUE or DRAMATIC MONOLOGUE is a speech by one character with an unseen, listening audience assumed. The speaker addresses himself or herself to the listener or listeners—possibly the reader or a silent character. "Porphyria's Lover" by Robert Browning is an easily available example.

The third literary form, the SOLILOQUY, is similar to the monologue, but the speaker is assumed to be alone, and his/her speech consists of private thoughts put into words:

The Dream

I dreamed I saw myself lie dead,
   And that my bed my coffin grew;
Silence and sleep this strange sight bred,
   But waked, I found I loved anew.
Looking next morn on your bright face,
   My eyes bequeathed my heart fresh pain;
A dart rushed in with every grace,
   And so I killed myself again:
O eyes, what shall distressed lovers do,
If open you can kill, if shut you view?
        —WILLIAM CARTWRIGHT

An ECLOGUE is a short pastoral dialogue, monologue, or soliloquy.

DROIGHNEACH *(dráiy-nach)*

Irish. Syllabic. A loose STANZA form. The single line can consist of from nine to thirteen syllables, and it always ends in a trisyllabic word. There is rhyming between lines one (1) and three (3), two (2) and four (4), etc. There are at least two cross-rhymes in each couplet, and alliteration in each line— usually the final word of the line alliterates with the preceding stressed word, and it always does so in the last line of each stanza. Stanzas can consist of any number of quatrains.

The poem (not the stanza) ends with the same first syllable, word, or line with which it begins. A possible scheme would be:

lines	syllables and rhymes	lines	syllables and rhymes
1.	x x b x x x x (x x a)	5.	x x x x x d x x (x x c)
2.	x x x x a x x x (x x b)	6.	x x x c x x x x x x (x x d)
3.	x x x x x b (x x a)	7.	x x d x x x x x x (x x c)
4.	x x x x a x x (x x b)	8.	x x x x c x (x x d)

ECHO VERSE

Any verse form written so that the last few words or syllables, when repeated at the end of each line, form a response to the line, as in the example given in the section on the BREF DOUBLE, "Bref Double à l'Écho." In that poem, it is possible for the repeated words to be read as a separate poem that responds to the main poem as a whole, in addition to the individual lines.

Another form of echo verse is DIMINISHING VERSE, in which letters or sounds are deleted from the first part of the last word in successive lines of each stanza:

Paradise

I bless thee, lord, because I *grow*
Among thy trees, which in a *row*
To thee both fruit and order *owe.*

What open force, or hidden *charm*
Can blast my fruit, or bring me *harm,*
While the inclosure is thine *arm?*

Inclose me still for fear I *start.*
Be to me rather sharp and *tart,*
Than let me want thy hand and *art.*

When thou dost greater judgements *spare,*
And with thy knife but prune and *pare,*
Even fruitful trees more fruitful *are.*

Such sharpness shows the sweetest *friend:*
Such cuttings rather heal than *rend:*
And such beginnings touch their *end.*

—GEORGE HERBERT

ECLOGUE—*see* BUCOLICS, DRAMATICS.

ECLOGUE DEBAT

A form of BUCOLICS, DIDACTICS, DRAMATICS, and FORENSICS, this form is an argument between country lovers. The example here is written in HYMNAL OCTAVE (see COMMON MEASURE):

Robin and Makyn

Robin sat on a good green hill,
Keeping a flock was he,
Merry Makyn near him till,
"Robin, have ruth for me;
I have loved thee loud and still
For years now two or three,
Doleful in secret; unless thou will,
I fear I shall doubtless die."

Robin answered, "By the Rood,
Nothing of love I know
But keeping my sheep under yon wood—
Lo! where they wander a-row:
What has marred thee in thy mood,
Makyn, I beg thou show;
Or what is love, or to be loved?
Fain would I learn that law."

"At love's lair, to learn its lore
Take there this a-b-c:
Be kind, courteous, and fair as fair,
Wise, generous, hearty
So that thou need not to endure
What hidden hurts may harm thee;
Fight thy pain with all thy power,
Have patience and be privy."

Robin answered her again,
"I know not what is love,
But I am marvelous uncertain
What makes thee thus to grieve:

The weather is fair, I have no pain,
My hale sheep climb above;
And should we play upon this plain,
We both would earn reproof."

"Robin, pay heed unto my tale,
Work all as I have said,
And thou shalt have my heart all hale,
Aye, and my maidenhead.
Since God sends thee beauty for bale,
And mourning is remade,
I plead with thee, if I turn tail,
Doubtless I am but dead."

"Makyn, this morning it may betide,
While ye waylay me here,
My sheep may hap to stray aside
While we have lain full near;
I fret this moment as I bide
That they shall disappear—
What freights my heart I will not hide;
Makyn, be of good cheer."

"Robin, thou rob my ruth and rest;
I love but thee alone."
"Makyn, adieu, the sun goes west,
The day is nearly gone."
"Robin, I grieve; I am distressed
That love will be my bane."
"Go love, Makyn, wherever thou list,
For mistresses I want none."

"Robin, I stand in such a stall;
I sigh, and that full sore."
"Makyn, I have been here this while;
At home God grant I were."
"My honey, Robin, talk awhile,
If thou wilt do no more."
"Makyn, some other man beguile,
For homeward I will fare."

Upon his own way Robin went
Light as the leaf of a tree;
Makyn, spited of her intent,
Watched Robin across the lea
And vowed to spurn him without stint.
Then Makyn cried out on high,
"Now may thou sing, for I am spent!
What ails this love in me?"

Makyn went home and did not fail,
Weary of learning to weep.
Then Robin in a full-fair dale
Gathered together his sheep,
When some part of what made Makyn ail
Into his heart did creep;
He followed her fast till he could hale
And tell her, "Take good keep!

"Abide, abide, thou fair Makyn,
One word for anything;
For all my love, it shall be thine,
Without any departing.
O take my heart, for to have thine
Is all my coveting;
My sheep till tomorrow's hours nine
Will need of no keeping."

"Robin, thou has heard sing and say
In gestes and stories old,
The man that will not when he may
Shall have not when he would.
I pray that Jesus every day
Increase their cares and cold
Who shall contend with thee to play
By firth, forest, or fold."

"Makyn, the night is soft and dry,
The weather is warm and fair,
And the greenwood is here nearby,
We may walk privy where
No gossips will be near to spy

Upon our trysting there;
Therein, Makyn, both ye and I,
Unseen we may repair."

"Robin, that world is all away
And quite brought to an end,
And never again after today
Shall I come as thou wend;
For of my pain thou made but play,
Vainly did my bough bend;
As thou hast done, so shall I say,
'Mourn on, *I* think to mend.'"

"Makyn, the hope of all my weal,
My heart on thee is set,
And ever to thee shall I kneel
While I have blood to let;
Never to fail, as others fail,
Whatever grace I get."
"Robin, with thee I will not deal;
Adieu, for thus we met."

Makyn went home, blithe anew,
Across the forest floor;
Robin mourned, and Makyn flew,
She sang, he sighed full sore;
And so she left him woe and rue
In care and in dolor,
Keeping his herd beside a sleugh
Upon the forest floor.

—ROBERT HENRYSON

EDDA MEASURES

Norse. Accentual. There are three EDDA MEASURES, all of
which are alliterative (similar to ANGLO-SAXON PROSODY):

OLD STORY MEASURE is a QUATRAIN STANZA, each stich of
which has four stresses, split by a central caesura into two
hemistichs of two stresses each. The third stressed syllable in
each line *always* alliterates with *either or both of the first two
stressed syllables;* the fourth stressed syllable *never* does, al-

though it may cross-alliterate with the following line. In each hemistich there are two, sometimes three, unstressed syllables. A possible scheme would be:

lines	stresses, alliterations, caesurae
1.	b́ x b́ x · x b́ ć x
2.	d́ x x f́ · x d́ x ǵ
3.	x h́ x j́ · j́ x ḱ x
4.	x x ḱ ḱ · x ḱ x í x

SPEECH MEASURE is a QUATRAIN STANZA, each line of which has four stresses, split by a central caesura into two hemistichs of two stresses each. The third stressed syllable in each line *always* alliterates with *either or both* of the *first two stressed syllables;* the fourth stressed syllable *never* does, though it may cross-alliterate with the following line. In each hemistich there are *three* or *four unstressed* syllables:

1.	b́ x x ć x · x ć x x d́ x
2.	x f́ x x ǵ · x f́ x x h́
3.	h́ x x x ḿ · x ḿ x x h́ x
4.	x ḿ x ḿ x · x ḿ x x ń x

SONG MEASURE is also a QUATRAIN STANZA. Lines one (1) and three (3) have four stresses, split by a central caesura into two hemistichs of two stresses each. The third stressed syllable in these lines *always* alliterates with *either or both* of the first two stressed syllables; the fourth stressed syllable *never* does, though it may cross-alliterate with the following line. In each hemistich there may be two or three unstressed syllables.

Lines two (2) and four (4) of the quatrain contain three stressed syllables, two of which alliterate. There is no caesura, and there are up to four unstressed syllables in the line. The scheme for the form would be:

1.   b́ x x ć · ć x x d́ x

2.   x x f́ x x f́ g

3.   x h́ x j́ · h́ x ḱ

4.   x ḱ x x í x í

In the following example of song measure, some liberties have been taken with the form:

The Monks' Massacre
From the Anglo-Saxon Chronicle for the Year 1083

Those were drear days and dire
   At the abbey of Glastonbury
When Thurstan came from Caen to become
   Abbot of the English monks.
But a little wit and less wisdom
   Had the Abbot Thurstan.
In many matters he misruled the monks—
   They suffered at first in stillness.
At last they complained in a kindly way,
   Asked him to rule them rightly;
They would be steadfast in all he asked
   if the abbot would but love them.
Thurstan would think no thoughts of the sort,
   But made them give up St. Gregory
And chant his French chansos instead—
   The foolish songs of Fécamp.
He treated them woefully, threatened worse
   Till one day he went into chapter
And spoke against them, swore to ill-treat them.
   He called for his layman knights
Who fell on the monks fully armed—
   The monks were stricken to stone,
Bewildered at first, fearful and helpless
   Before the furious onslaught.
At last they scattered—some of them fled
   From chapter into the church.
They heaved the doors hard-to behind them
   And shot the bolts in the locks.

The French knights followed the monks
   Into the monastery, meaning
To drag them forth, for they dared not go
   To face the abbot's henchmen.
But a heavy thing happened that day:
   The French forced the choir
And threw missiles at the monks below
   Gathered about the altar,
And some from above, in the upper storey,
   Shot arrows altarward
Where the wretched monks writhed
   Beneath the shaft-struck cross.
Some cried to God and crept beneath
   The altar, asking of Him
The mercy their fellow men denied them.
   Yet more fiercely the French
Shot their shafts and, shouting, broke
   Down the doors of the chapel,
Killed some monks and wounded more
   Till, spilling down
Out from under the altar of God,
   The blood of the brothers flowed
About the boots of the brave French
   And their thirsty abbot Thurstan.

            —ANONYMOUS

ELEGIAC COUPLET, ELEGIAC DISTICH—*see* ELEGIACS.

ELEGIACS

Greek. Quantitative accentual-syllabics. A COUPLET mea-
sure. The first line is a CLASSICAL HEXAMETER: the *first four feet*
are either spondees or dactyls, the fifth foot is a dactyl, the
sixth is a spondee. The second line of the couplet is a CLASSI-
CAL PENTAMETER, consisting, in this order, of two dactyls, a
spondee, and two anapests. It can be rhymed or unrhymed.
A possible scheme would be:

lines   *meters*
1.   ˈ   ˈ   ˈ   ˈ   ˈ   ˈˈ
      xxx xxx xxx xxx xxx xx

2.   ˈ   ˈ   ˈˈ   ˈ   ˈ
      xxx xxx xx xxx xxx

A Talisman
For Dave McLean

Lead for this talisman. Pure, so that Saturn will live in it. Pure
                                                              lead.
Both of its faces are rubbed smooth. On its front, in a star
pentagram, cut with a diamond burin a scythe so that Nabam,
    standing upon his demoniac pedestal Tau, shall be laid low—
old as he is—by Oriphiel, angel of Saturday. Jesus,
    nailed to a T, is the capstone of this coin made of lead,
though he will never appear in his person, but only as
                                                          backdrop.
Grave on the opposite face this, in a six-pointed star:
REMPHA, surrounding the head of a bull. Without witnesses
                                                        carve your
    talisman. Wear it in good health. It will keep you from death,
frighten the devil of cancer, leukemia—rot of the white bone.
    Marrow will redden. Wear this! It will save you and me.
Bear it—your talisman; wear it, my brother. Or carry this
                                                            poem,
    Dies Saturni, to life's end. It is all I can do.

                                              —WESLI COURT

Elegiacs was the classical meter in which elegies were
written. An elegy is a mournful song, a reflection on the
passing of time or on death. See also the ELEGY and PASTORAL
ELEGY in the section on LYRICS. Richard Moore's "Friends"
and Miller Williams' "For Victor Jara" in *Strong Measures*
(op. cit.) are other examples of contemporary elegiacs.

ELEGY—*see* ELEGIACS.

ENCLOSED TERCET—*see* TERCET.

ENCLOSED TRIPLET—*see* TRIPLET.

ENGLISH ODE—*see* ODE.

ENGLISH SONNET—*see* SONNET.

ENGLYNS *(én-glin)*
Welsh. Syllabic. There are eight types of englyns. Six of them, those treated in this section, are QUATRAIN STANZAS.

ENGLYN CYRCH (én-glin kirch) has seven syllables in each line. Lines one (1) and two (2) turn on a single rhyme. Line three (3) cross-rhymes into one of the three central syllables of line four (4):

lines	syllables and rhymes
1.	x x x x x x a
2.	x x x x x x a
3.	x x x x x x b
4.	x x *x x b* x a

Gnomic Verses

Frost shall freeze, fire will eat wood,
Ice will bridge and the earth brood.
Water shall wear winter's shield,
Yet the field will be renewed.

Frost's fetters shall free the grain,
Wonderlock will yield to rain,
And there shall be fair weather
When the winter goes to wane.

Sunwarmed summer! What was dumb
Shall find voice. The body, numb
When the deep wave was most dark,
Will feel when the lark has come.
                    —ANONYMOUS

Each line of ENGLYN LLEDDFBROEST (én-glin llédd-uhv-broyst) *diphthong-rhymes* with the others and has a count of seven syllables. In Welsh, the rhymes used were the four diphthongs *ae, oe, wy,* and *ei.* Since this structure is impossible to reproduce in English, any *similar diphthongs* can be substituted and can be considered to rhyme with one another. Here is a one stanza schematic:

lines	syllables and diphthong rhymes
1.	x x x x x x oe
2.	x x x x x x wy
3.	x x x x x x ei
4.	x x x x x x ae

ENGLYN PROEST DALGRON (én-glin proyst dál-gron) has seven syllables in each line. All the lines consonate with one another on vowels or similar diphthongs:

The Grave

Everyman comes to the dank earth.
Folk, forlorn and small, perish.
What wealth rears is wracked by death.
In an hour dirt devoureth.

Great maw, end of what I clutch,
What I loved you turn to filth.
Mine will be a chill stone hearth—
Life was not meant for a youth.

Each man's cold estate is death;
He walks alone on the heath
That will take him in its clinch,
Come at last to the cromlech.

—DAFYDD BENFRAS

In ENGLYN PROEST GADWYNOG (én-glin proyst ga-dóy-nog), each line has seven syllables. Lines one (1) and three (3) rhyme; lines two (2) and four (4) consonate with lines one (1) and three (3) and with each other:

lines	syllables, consonances, and rhymes
1.	x x x x x x r
2.	x x x x x x or
3.	x x x x x x r
4.	x x x x x x or

ENGLYN UNODL CRWCA (én-glin éen-oddle créw-cah) has lines with syllable counts of seven, seven, ten, and six (7–7–10–6), respectively. Lines one (1), two (2), and four (4) end with the *main* rhyme. In line three (3), the main rhyme is followed by one, two, or three syllables that are echoed by assonance, alliteration, or secondary rhyme in the first part of the *fourth* line:

lines	syllables and rhymes
1.	x x x x x x A
2.	x x x x x x A
3.	x x x x x x A x x b
4.	*x b x* x x A

ENGLYN UNODL UNION (én-glin éen-oddle éen-yon) merely shifts the positions of the two couplets that make up englyn unodl crwca: lines three (3) and four (4) of the latter become lines one (1) and two (2), and lines one (1) and two (2) become lines three (3) and four (4) of the englyn unodl union.

ENVELOPE, ENVELOPE STANZA—*see* QUATRAIN.

ENVOI

An envoi, or envoy, was originally the concluding half-stanza of verse forms such as the BALLADE or the CHANT ROYAL. One of its traditional functions was to provide the de-nouement for what had been said in the body of the poem, or to apostrophize it and send it on its way to its intended audience.

Detached from the verse form for which it was a tail or coda, the envoi retains its function as a dedication. For an example, see Chaucer's "Complaint to His Purse" in the section on the BALLADE.

EPIC—*see* NARRATIVES.

EPICEDIUM

An ELEGY for the dead delivered by a chorus. See OBSEQUY.

EPIGRAM—*see* SATIRICS.

EPISTLE—*see* DIDACTICS *and* SOMONKA.

EPITAPH—*see* SATIRICS.

EPITHALAMION, EPITHALAMIUM—*see* LYRICS.

EPYLLION

A "little EPIC," originally composed in dactylic hexameter verse. See NARRATIVES.

EVENSONG

A formal lyric prayer to be sung in the evening. See LITURGICS.

FABLE, FABLIAU—*see* DIDACTICS *and* NARRATIVES.

FLYTING—*see* FORENSICS.

FOLK BALLAD—*see* BALLAD.

FORENSICS

Forensics is the minor poetic subgenre of debate and argument. Several forms are associated with it, including the DEBAT, in which opposing parties contend (see Robert Henryson's "Robin and Makyn" under ECLOGUE DEBAT).

A set Spanish form of the debate is the PREGUNTA, in which one poet asks a question (*requesta*) or series of questions, and another gives the reply (*respuesta*) or series of replies. The following poem, written in the form of a pregunta, was penned by a single poet:

Upon Love, by Way of Question and Answer

I bring ye love, *Quest.* What will love do?
  Ans. Like, and dislike ye;
I bring ye love: *Quest.* What will love do?
  Ans. Stroke ye to strike ye;
I bring ye love: *Quest.* What will love do?
  Ans. Love will befool ye;
I bring ye love: *Quest.* What will love do?
  Ans. Heat ye to cool ye;
I bring ye love: *Quest.* What will love do?
  Ans. Love gifts will send ye:

I bring ye love: *Quest.* What will love do?
  Ans. Stock ye to spend ye;
I bring ye love: *Quest.* What will love do?
  Ans. Love will fulfill ye;
I bring ye love: *Quest.* What will love do?
  Ans. Kiss ye to kill ye.
      —ROBERT HERRICK

A Japanese form of question and answer is the KATAUTA, which is based on the *utterance:* a spontaneous, emotive word or phrase. Such an utterance formalized is the *basic* katauta—a question *or* its answer. "Am I in love?" is a katauta, as is its spontaneous and *intuitive* answer: "Birds are flying." A pair of such katautas, that is, a question plus its answer, is a MONDO:

Am I in love? Birds are flying.

Mondos can appear in parallel constructions of various kinds, as in this cross-parallel (see *chiasmus*) set:

Am I in love? Birds are flying.
Do birds fly? I am in love.

To the Occidental eye, this verse looks much like a *syllogism*—

Grass is green.
Bluegrass is grass.
Bluegrass is green.

The katauta answer, however, is not logical, it is intuitive. This point is important, for although Western arguments are based in rational thinking, certain kinds of Oriental debate are based on intuition, as for instance in Zen Buddhism.

A set form of the KATAUTA consists of three parts arranged in lines of 5–7–7 syllables, unrhymed:

lines	syllables
1.	x x x x x
2.	x x x x x x x
3.	x x x x x x x

The line-lengths are approximately breath-length (like William Carlos Williams' American equivalent of this system—his "breath-pause" concept of line-phrasing where each line equals one phrase—see the TRIVERSEN) or the appropriate lengths to ask a sudden, emotive question and respond to it, also emotively. Seventeen or nineteen syllables are therefore about as many as can normally be uttered in one short breath; five to seven syllables are approximately equal to the utterance of a question or its answer.

In Williams' *variable accentuals* variation of this concept (he called it the "variable foot," which is misleading since no "verse foot," strictly speaking, is involved), two to four *stresses* are approximately equal to an utterance, and six to twelve accents are as many as can be uttered in a short breath. Thus, in Williams' prosody, each line is a phrase of about two to four stresses, and three lines equal a clause of about six to twelve stresses. Williams' system, however, does not necessarily have anything to do with questions and answers.

The three-line KATAUTA is the basic and organic unit of Japanese syllabic poetry, which culminated in the development of the HAIKU. Here is a poem that illustrates some of the Japanese syllabic forms, while it parallels the development of the forms leading up to the haiku:

Paradigm

> *Why does the brook run?*
> The banks of the stream are green.   } MONDO

> *Why does the stream run?*
> The banks of the brook bloom
> with roe and cup-moss, with rue.   } KATAUTA

The trees are filled with
cups. Grain in the fields, straw men
    talking with the wind.
Have you come far, water-
borne, wind-born? Here are
hounds-tongue and mistletoe oak.

CHOKA

When the spears bend as
you walk through vervain or broom,
    call out to the brook—
it will swell in your veins as
you move through broom and vervain.

WAKA
(5–7, 5–7, 7)

Have you spoken aloud? Here,
where the swallows' crewel-work
sews the sky with mist?
You must cut the filament.
You must be the lone spider.

TANKA
(5–7–5, 7–7)

—L. T.

Other Western forms of the debate are the BRAG or BOAST,
in which two speakers try to outdo each other in outrageous
claims about their own greatness, and the Scottish FLYTING,
in which two poets attempt to demolish each other with in-
sults and invective.

GENETHLIACUM

An occasional poem written in honor of a birth; see ODE.

GEORGICS—*see* DIDACTICS.

GESTE

A story in verse; see ROMANCE.

GLOSE

Spanish and Portuguese. Usually accentual-syllabic. Can be
written in any prosody or line-length, though each line is
usually of a single length. "Glose" means *gloss,* a "commen-
tary" upon something; in this case, upon quoted lines that

appear as a headnote or *epigraph* at the beginning of the poem. This epigraph is called the *texte;* each line of the texte becomes a *repeton,* a refrain that appears just one other time in the body of the poem. The first line of the texte finishes stanza one, the second line, stanza two, and so on until the texte is exhausted and the poem comes to an end.

Here is a diagram of a glose written on a two-line texte in quatrain stanzas:

lines	rhymes and repetons		lines	rhymes and repetons
1.	A ⎫	*texte*	7.	d
2.	B ⎭		8.	b
3.	c		9.	d
4.	a		10.	B
5.	c			
6.	A			

The following poem is a DOUBLE GLOSE—that is, each texte line is used twice. It is written in the form of a STAVE:

Western Wind

Western wind, when wilt thou blow,
That the small rain down shall rain?
Christ! that my love were in my arms,
And I in my bed again.
                    —ANONYMOUS

Western wind, when wilt thou blow?
When shall the rivers begin to flow
Over this ice toward the sea?
When will the branches of the tree
Drop their mantles of rime and snow?
Western wind, when wilt thou blow,

That the small rain down shall rain?
Then may the willows in their train
Loosen their limbs upon the stream;
Then may birdsong burst this dream
Of winter to seek the sprouting grain,
That the small rain down shall rain.

Christ! that my love were in my arms
Where the grass greens and the bee swarms!
She is fair as the mountain heather,
Comely and kind as Maytime's weather
Over the land after April storms—
Christ! that my love were in my arms,

And I in my bed again
Where gladly I have slept and lain
Upon the pillow of her hair.
When shall I once more come there,
Her breast beneath the counterpane,
And I in my bed again?

—WESLI COURT

For another glose, see "Simon Judson" in *Strong Measures* (op. cit.).

GWAWDODYNS *(gwow-dód-in)*

Gwawdodyn, a syllabic Welsh form, is a QUATRAIN STANZA with lines of nine, nine, ten, and nine (9–9–10–9) syllables, respectively. The first, second, and fourth lines end-rhyme with one another. The third line may rhyme internally with itself, or there may be a syllable *before the end of the line* that rhymes *into* line four.

Here are two possible stanza schemes:

lines	syllables and rhymes
1.	x x x x x x x x a
2.	x x x x x x x x a
3.	x x x b x x x x b
4.	x x x x x x x x a

The second method, which is looser, might be plotted this way:

1.	x x x x x x x x a
2.	x x x x x x x x a
3.	x x x x x x b x x x
4.	x x x b x x x x a

The GWAWDONYN HIR (gwow-dód-in heer) is similar except that a rhyming quatrain, each line of which contains nine syllables, is substituted for the opening couplet. Thus, instead of two lines rhyming *aa*, there are four lines rhyming *aaaa* beginning the stanza, which then becomes a SESTET.

HAIKAI NO RENGA—*see the* RENGA *in the section on the* TANKA.

HAIKU

The haiku is a Japanese tercet. Its lines consist of five, seven, and five syllables, respectively. It is generally unrhymed:

lines	syllables
1.	x x x x x
2.	x x x x x x x
3.	x x x x x

The word HOKKU is Chinese in origin, and in Japanese poetry it came to specify the *first triplet* of a RENGA CHAIN. This first verse set the theme of the chain and was the most important part of the poem, the rest ringing changes upon and elaborating the hokku. The hokku of a renga chain ended with a full stop—it was complete in and of itself.

A distinction has been made between the SENRYU and the haiku, though both have exactly the same external form. The senryu is "An inquiry into the nature of Man"; the haiku, "An inquiry into the nature of the Universe."

By various stages the term haiku came to denote an independent tercet of 5–7–5 syllables. Based originally on the KATAUTA, and later derived from both the RENGA and the TANKA, the haiku dropped all glosses, comments, or elaborations. It became a poem based on image, emotive utterance, and certain other characteristics as well: spareness, condensation, spontaneity and ellipsis, plus a seasonal element—they are about spring, summer, fall, or winter. Ideally, the haiku, though complete in itself, is open-ended in that its statement reverberates beyond the poem into overtone.

The haiku is philosophically an outgrowth of Zen Buddhism. Haiku translated into English tend to appear, to Western eyes, overly sentimental and to fall victim to the pathetic fallacy—overstated personification. We do not understand that the Zen poet is trying to put himself or herself into the place of the thing perceived, empathizing with the inanimate object. Moreover, the Zen poet is trying to *become one* with the object and thus with all things.

The haiku has perhaps best been described as "A moment of intense perception." William Carlos Williams enunciated the American-British imagist doctrine as "No ideas but in things." Both conceptions are, if not identical, at least quite similar, for both are based upon the sensory level. Williams' dictum and T. S. Eliot's "objective correlative" sever the observer from the perceived object, while at the same time preserving much of the *effect* of Zen empathy. An objective correlative is simply the vehicle of a metaphor. The theory is that, if the correct object that correlates with the idea to be expressed (symbolizes that idea) is chosen, then the idea will arise through connotation and overtone without being stated denotatively. It is through this objectivity, finally, that the poet in English achieves empathy—which is only a way of saying there is no such thing as pure objectivity. Here are fourteen English versions of Japanese haiku:

Fourteen Haiku

Will it soon be spring?
They lay the ground-work for it,
the plum tree and moon.

One sees in the glass
mere glass, not quicksilver, not
spring in the plum tree.

On the mountain path
they arise at once—the scent
of plums and the sun!

The hollyhocks turn
to follow the sun's footpath
through the rains of May.

The winds blow cherry
petals from all four quarters
to the lake's currents.

I would lie down drunk
on a bed of stone covered
with soft pinks blooming.

Bush-clover spills not
one drop of white dew, although
its waves never still.

The bell's chiming fades;
scent blossoms from the echo
of evening shadow.

The lightning flickers;
still darkness follows the voice
of the night-heron.

Please come to visit,
for I am lonely. One leaf
falls from the kiri.

The wind of autumn
is sharp in the chestnut tree,
yet its burrs are green.

Leaning on their canes
a snow-haired family comes
to visit the graves.

Grave, shake you as well
as my quaking voice in this
chill wind of the fall.

No one walks this road
on which I travel, on which
autumn darkness falls.

—BASHŌ

The following poem is an example of the SENRYU; it is a cento on lines from Emily Dickinson's letters.

An Amherst Haiku

　　Will you bring me a
jacinth for every finger,
　　and an onyx shoe?

For a poem that traces some of the development of Japanese poetry to the haiku, see "Paradigm" in the section on FORENSICS. See the UTTERANCE, the MONDO and the two forms of KATAUTA in the same section; for related forms see also TANKA and RENGA.

HENDECASYLLABICS
Greek. Quantitative accentual syllabics. A pentameter *line* of eleven syllables. Strictly, it is made up, in this order, of a trochee or spondee, a dactyl, and three trochees or two trochees and a spondee:

line　　　　*meters*
　　　　′ ′ ′ ′ ′
　I.　　xx xxx xx xx xx

or:
　　　　′ ′ ′ ′ ′ ′ ′
　2.　　xx xxx xx xx xx

For an example of hendecasyllabics, see the second half of Tennyson's "Milton" in the section on ALCAICS.

HEROIC COUPLET—*see* HEROICS.

HEROICS
English or Greek. Accentual-syllabic. The ENGLISH HEROIC LINE is iambic pentameter *blank verse*. A distich in this meter is called a HEROIC COUPLET. If the stanza is a QUATRAIN in this meter, it is called the HEROIC STANZA, set forms of which are

the ITALIAN and the SICILIAN QUATRAIN. The Italian and Sicilian OCTAVES and OTTAVA RIMA are HEROIC OCTAVES.

The CLASSICAL HEROIC LINE is the hexameter (see ELEGIACS). Verses composed in either of these meters are called HEROIC VERSE. Traditionally, the greatest heroic form is the EPIC (see NARRATIVES), a poem of great length dealing with matters of large import and grand proportion.

Because the most famous poems written in heroic couplets are too long to fit into this volume, only a sample of a lesser known poem is given here, and the reader is referred to the works of Alexander Pope, the most famous practitioner of the form, John Dryden, and others.

Description of an Author's Bedchamber

Where the Red Lion, staring o'er the way,
Invites each passing stranger that can pay;
Where Calvert's butt, and Parsons' black champagne,
Regale the drabs and bloods of Drury Lane;
There in a lonely room, from bailiffs snug,
The Muse found Scroggen stretched beneath a rug.
A window, patched with paper, lent a ray
That dimly showed the state in which he lay;
The sanded floor that grits beneath the tread,
The humid wall with paltry pictures spread;
The royal game of goose was there in view,
And the Twelve Rules the royal martyr drew;
The Seasons, framed with listing, found a place,
And brave Prince William showed his lampblack face.
The morn was cold; he views with keen desire
The rusty grate unconscious of a fire:
With beer and milk arrears the frieze was scored,
And five cracked teacups dressed the chimney board;
A nightcap decked his brows instead of bay,
A cap by night—a stocking all the day.
                                        —OLIVER GOLDSMITH

HIR A THODDAID *(heer ah thódd-eyed)*
Welsh. Syllabic. A SESTET STANZA. Line five has a count of ten syllables. The other five lines each contain nine syllables. Lines one (1), two (2), three (3), four (4), and six (6) rhyme. A syllable toward the end of line five (5) cross-rhymes into the middle of line six (6):

lines	syllables and rhymes
1.	x x x x x x x x a
2.	x x x x x x x x a
3.	x x x x x x x x a
4.	x x x x x x x x a
5.	x x x x x x *x b x x*
6.	x x x *b x x* x x a

HOKKU—*see* HAIKU.

HYMNAL OCTAVE, HYMNAL STANZA—*see* COMMON MEASURE.

IDYL—*see* BUCOLICS.

INCANTATION—*see* LITURGICS.

IN MEMORIAM STANZA—*see* ENVELOPE STANZA.

INTERLUDE
A short play, often satiric or comic in nature, performed between the acts of a longer play, usually a tragedy. A PLAMPEDE is a satiric interlude performed between the acts of a comedy.

IRREGULAR ODE—*see* ODE.

ITALIAN OCTAVE—*see* OCTAVE.

ITALIAN SESTET, ITALIAN SONNET—*see* SONNET.

KATAUTA—*see* FORENSICS.

KEATSIAN ODE—*see* ENGLISH ODE.

KYRIELLE

French. Syllabic. A poem written in QUATRAIN STANZAS. Each line has a count of eight syllables. The last line of the first quatrain is the refrain, and it reappears as the last line of each quatrain. Usually it is rhymed. The poem can have any number of stanzas:

lines	syllables and rhymes	lines	syllables and rhymes
1.	x x x x x x x a	5.	x x x x x x x c
2.	x x x x x x x b	6.	x x x x x x x b
3.	x x x x x x x a	7.	x x x x x x x c
4.	x x x x x x x B—*refrain*	8.	x x x x x x x B—*refrain*

For an example of a kyrielle, see Theodore Roethke's "Dirty Dinky" in *Strong Measures* (op. cit.).

LAI

A French form or stanza pattern. Syllabic. A poem or STANZA of nine lines turning on two rhymes: *aabaabaab*. The *a* lines are five syllables long; the *b* lines are two syllables long.

In a poem consisting of more than one stanza, the following stanzas have their own rhymes. A diagram for one stanza is thus:

lines	syllables and rhymes
1.	x x x x a
2.	x x x x a
3.	x b
4.	x x x x a
5.	x x x x a
6.	x b
7.	x x x x a
8.	x x x x a
9.	x b

The LAI NOUVEAU, also French and syllabic, is a development of the lai. More complicated than the lai, the opening *a* lines of the lai nouveau form a refrain for later stanzas, while alternating (as in the VILLANELLE). The A^1 line closes stanza two, A^2 closes stanza three, and so on to the last stanza, where they are united in a couplet *in reverse order* to close the poem: A^2A^1. Though the *main* rhyme is usually carried from stanza to stanza, sometimes the short-line rhymes vary from stanza to stanza.

It should be noted that the two-syllable, rhyming lines are extremely difficult to do in English. The schematic for a strict poem consisting of two, eight-line stanzas can be plotted thus:

lines	syllables, rhymes, refrains	lines	syllables, rhymes, refrains
1.	x x x x A^1—*refrain*	9.	x x x x a
2.	x x x x A^2—*refrain*	10.	x x x x a
3.	x b	11.	x c
4.	x x x x a	12.	x x x x a
5.	x x x x a	13.	x x x x a
6.	x b	14.	x c
7.	x x x x a	15.	x x x x A^2
8.	x x x x a	16.	x x x x A^1

The VIRELAI, like its sister forms, is a syllabic French stanza pattern. Its syllabic count is the same as the lai, and it has, as a rule, nine lines to the stanza, as does the lai. The difference is that the *long* lines of a following stanza pick up the short-line rhymes of the preceding stanza. This *interlocking* can be carried on indefinitely until the final stanza picks up as its short-line rhyme the long-line rhyme of the *first* stanza. For other interlocking forms, see the RUBAIYAT and TERZA RIMA.

LAMENT—*see* LYRICS.

LAY—*see* LYRICS.

LIMERICK

French. Originally syllabic but, in English, quantitative accentual-syllabics. A single QUINTET, rhyming *aabba* and written in iambic and anapestic measures. Lines one (1), two

(2), and five (5) have an iamb and two anapests, in that order; lines three (3) and four (4) have either an iamb and an anapest or two anapests. Line five (5) can be merely a modified repetition of line one (1). Most of the best limericks are anonymous and scurrilous, in fact, pornographic. Here is the schematic:

lines	meters and rhymes
1.	x x́ x x x́ x x́a *or* A
2.	x x́ x x x́ x x́a
3.	x x́ x x b́
4.	x x́ x x b́
5.	x x́ x x x́ x x́a *or* A

Old Man with a Beard

There was an Old Man with a beard
Who said, "It is just as I feared!—
 Two Owls and a Hen,
 Four Larks and a Wren,
Have all built their nests in my beard!"

—EDWARD LEAR

The French ancestry of the limerick has been disputed. Some authorities feel it is a native English form, descended from the MADSONG STANZA, which in turn is traced from the main stanza pattern of the medieval "The Cuckoo Song," given here in a modern version:

The Cuckoo Song

Sing cuckoo now! Sing cuckoo!
Sing cuckoo! Sing cuckoo now!

Summer is a-coming in,
Loudly sing cuckoo!
 It grows the seed
 And blows the mead,
And springs the wood anew—

> Sing cuckoo!
The ewe bleats after the lamb,
And after the calf, the cow;
> The bullock starts,
> The buck farts—
Merry sing cuckoo!

> Cuckoo, cuckoo!
> Well sing ye, cuckoo,
> Nor cease ye never, now!
> —ANONYMOUS

However, the French background of this form is probably not disputable, because it is clearly a podic form, and podics, as we have seen in the chapter on the sonic level, developed after Chaucer adapted French syllabic verse to English accentual verse and adopted Norman rhyming.

The rhyme scheme of madsong stanza is that of "The Cuckoo Song" main stanza, $a^3b^3c^2c^2b^3$, and, like it, the meters are podic. Often the lines consonate rather than rhyme. The long lines often end in an extra unaccented syllable (falling endings). Here is the schematic of the first stanza of "Tom O'Bedlam's Song," which follows:

lines   stresses and rhymes
1.   x x x x x x x a
2.   x x x x x x b
3.   x x x x x c
4.   x x x x c
5.   x x x x x x x b

The madsong itself, aside from the stanza pattern (and again like "The Cuckoo Song"), is a lyric sung by a fool or a madman:

Tom O'Bedlam's Song

From the hag and hungry goblin
That into rags would rend ye,
    All the spirits that stand
    By the naked man
In the book of moons defend ye!

I slept not since the Conquest;
Till then I never wakéd
    Till the roguish boy
    Of love, where I lay,
Me found, and stripped me naked.

The moon's my constant mistress,
And the lonely owl my marrow;
    The flaming drake,
    And the night-crow, make
Me music, to my sorrow.

I know more than Apollo,
For, oft when he lies sleeping,
    I behold the stars
    At mortal wars,
And the rounded welkin weeping.

The moon embraces her shepherd,
And the queen of love her warrior;
    While the first doth horn
    The stars of morn,
And the next the heavenly farrier.

With a host of furious fancies
Whereof I am commander;
    With a burning spear,
    And a horse of air,
To the wilderness I wander.

With a knight of ghosts and shadows,
I summoned am to tourney
    Ten leagues beyond
    The wide world's end;
Methinks it is no journey.

                    —ANONYMOUS

For a modern madsong in madsong stanza, see Wesli Court's "Odds Bodkin's Springsong" in *Poetry: An Introduction* (op. cit.). Not all madsongs, however, are written in this stanza pattern—see Yeats' "Crazy Jane and the Bishop" in the same book (where it is analyzed).

Despite the popularity of the limerick in the twentieth century, the older folk tradition of the madsong can still be found in current use. Here is a children's game song that was current at least as late as the 1940s:

Street Song

Help! Murder! Police!
My mother fell in the grease!
  I laughed so hard
  I fell in the lard.
Help! Murder! Police!
          —ANONYMOUS

Many experiments have been enacted with the limerick form. Among other things, it has been used with some success as a stanza pattern rather than as a poem form. Changing its hard and wrenched rhymes to consonances, however, produces strange results:

A Robbery

Some thieves sacked the home of Miss Hughes
Who owned a remarkable nose.
  She cried, "Sirs! I shall sneeze
  And alert the police
If you don't get out of my house!"
          —ANONYMOUS

But the form has settled down into, at its mildest, salacious suggestiveness—

Hornblower

A boozing musician named Rock
Just loved to blow jazz on his sock.

In the midst of a riff
One day he got stiff
When he grabbed, not his foot, but his crock.
—ANONYMOUS

—and, at its worst, its worst:

A Butcher

There once was a butcher named Sims
Who married a woman of whims.
She said "No!" once too often,
So he bought her a coffin
And made farewell love to her limbs.
—ANONYMOUS

LITANY—*see* LITURGICS.

LITERARY BALLAD—*see* BALLAD.

LITERARY EPITAPH—*see* EPITAPH.

LITURGICS

Liturgics is the minor subgenre of poetry based on the forms of public worship in the Christian church. These forms range from prayer to sermon, and they include even such things as curses. The spectrum is too broad to do much more than give examples of a few of the forms; but examples of others will be found elsewhere in this book.

The ANTIPHON is a dialogue between choirs, one choir singing the *versicle,* the other singing the response:

"Canst Thou Draw?"
Job XLI: 1–7

Canst thou draw out Leviathan with an hook, or his tongue
with a cord which thou lettest down? Canst thou put an
hook into his nose? or bore his jaw through with a thorn?
Vain attempt!
Will he make many supplications unto thee?
Terrible words!
Will he make a covenant with thee?

Distressing covenant!
Or, wilt thou take him for a servant forever?
Dreadful servant!
Wilt thou play with him, as with a bird?
Dismal play!
Or wilt thou bind him for thy maidens?
Strong cord!
Shall thy companions make a banquet of him?
Mournful banquet!
Shall they part him among the merchants?
Deadly shares!
Canst thou fill his skin with barbed irons?
Hopeless attempt!
Or his head with fish spears?
Despairing thought!

—MANOAH BODMAN

A CANTICLE is a scriptural hymn for public worship. A LITANY is a public prayer of penitence led by the clergyman and responded to by the congregation:

His Litany, to the Holy Spirit

In the hour of my distress,
When temptation me oppress,
And when I my sins confess,
        Sweet Spirit comfort me!

When I lie within my bed,
Sick in heart, and sick in head,
And with doubts discomforted,
        Sweet Spirit comfort me!

When the house doth sigh and weep,
And the world is drowned in sleep,
Yet mine eyes the watch do keep;
        Sweet Spirit comfort me!

When the artless doctor sees
No one hope but of his fees,
And his skill runs on the lees,
        Sweet Spirit comfort me!

When his potion and his pill—
His, or none, or little skill—
Meet for nothing but to kill,
    Sweet Spirit comfort me!

When the passing bell doth toll
And the Furies in a shoal
Come to fright a parting soul,
    Sweet Spirit comfort me!

When the tapers now burn blue
And the comforters are few,
And that number more, than true,
    Sweet Spirit comfort me!

When the priest his last hath prayed,
And I nod to what is said
Because my speech is now decayed,
    Sweet Spirit comfort me!

When (God knows) I'm tossed about,
Either with despair or doubt,
Yet before the glass be out,
    Sweet Spirit comfort me!

When the Tempter me pursueth
With the sins of all my youth
And half damns me with untruth,
    Sweet Spirit comfort me!

When the flames and hellish cries
Fright mine ears and fright mine eyes,
And all terrors me surprise,
    Sweet Spirit comfort me!

When the Judgement is revealed,
And that opened which was sealed,
When to Thee I have appealed,
    Sweet Spirit comfort me!
        —ROBERT HERRICK

A CURSE is a devout wish that someone be sent to damnation or be scourged in this life:

*Warning to Travelers Seeking Accommodations at
Mr. de Ville's Inn*

May all that dread the cruel fiend of night
Keep on, and not at this cursed mansion light.
'Tis Hell; 'tis Hell! and De Villes here do dwell:
Here dwells the Devil—surely this's Hell.
Nothing but wants: a drop to cool your tongue
Can't be procured these cruel fiends among.
　　Plenty of horrid fiends among!
Plenty of horrid grins and looks severe,
Hunger and thirst, but pity's banished here—
The right hand keep, if Hell on Earth you fear!
　　　　　—SARAH KEMBLE KNIGHT

A PRAYER is sometimes not much different from a curse:

*Resentments Composed because of the Clamor
of Town Topers Outside My Apartment*

I ask thy aid, O potent Rum!
To charm these wrangling topers dumb.
Thou hast their giddy brains possessed—
The man confounded with the beast—
And I, poor I, can get no rest.
Intoxicate them with thy fumes:
O still their tongues till morning comes!
　　　　　—SARAH KEMBLE KNIGHT

INCANTATIONS are charms, spells, conjurations, and so
forth—the apparatus of sympathetic magic. Other forms are
associated with incantations, such as ACROSTICS, ANAGRAMS,
and RUNES. The BLESSING is a form of incantation:

A House Blessing

Saint Francis and Saint Benedight,
Bless this house from wicked wight,
From the nightmare and the goblin,
That is hight Good-fellow Robin;

Keep it from all evil spirits,
Fairies, weasels, rats, and ferrets,
  From curfew time
  To the next Prime.
    —WILLIAM CARTWRIGHT

A CHANT is a religious recitative that has a refrain:

The Mystery

I am the breeze breathed at sea,
I am the wave woven of ocean,
I am the soft sound of spume,
I am the bull of the seven battles,
I am the cormorant upon the cliff,
I am the spear of the sun striking,
I am the rose of the fairest rose.
I am the wild bull of war,
I am the salmon stroking the flood,
I am the mere upon the moor,
I am the rune of rare lore,
I am the tooth of the long lance,
I am He who fired the head.

Who emblazons the mountain-meeting?
Who heralds the moon's marches?
Who leads the sun to its lair?
I am the Word, I am the Eye.
    —AMERGIN

A CAROL originally was merely a joyous hymn, but the
term has come by tradition to apply specifically to hymns
about the Nativity, whether joyous or not. See CAROL STANZA
for a strict stanza form.

LONG HYMNAL OCTAVE, LONG HYMNAL STANZA,
  LONG MEASURE, LONG OCTAVE—*see* COMMON
  MEASURE.

LYRICS

A major subgenre of poetry, lyrics are songs. Lyrics are spe-
cific to the genre, whereas the other two major subgenres,
narratives and dramatics, are not. There are many kinds of
songs. In this section I will name some of them, but there are
many other lyric forms listed throughout this volume.

The ALBA or AUBADE is a love song whose setting is dawn.
Sometimes each stanza ends with the word "dawn." John
Donne's "The Sun Rising," treated earlier in these pages, is
an aubade. A related form is the REVEILLE:

An Hymn to the Morning

Attend my lays, ye ever honored nine,
Assist my labours, and my strains refine;
In smoothest numbers pour the notes along,
For bright Aurora now demands my song.

Aurora, hail, and all the thousand dyes,
Which deck thy progress through the vaulted skies;
The morn awakes, and wide extends her rays,
On every leaf the gentle zephyr plays;
Harmonious lays the feathered race resume,
Dart the bright eye, and shake the painted plume.

Ye shady groves, your verdant gloom display
To shield your poet from the burning day:
Calliope, awake the sacred lyre,
While thy fair sisters fan the pleasing fire:
The bowers, the gales, the variegated skies
In all their pleasures in my bosom rise.

See in the east the illustrious king of day!
His rising radiance drives the shades away—
But oh! I feel his fervid leaves too strong,
And scarce begun, concludes the abortive song.

—PHILLIS WHEATLEY

ANACREONTICS praise wine, women, and song:

Anacrontick Verse

Brisk methinks I am and fine,
When I drink my capering wine:

Then to love I do incline,
When I drink my wanton wine;
And I wish all maidens mine,
When I drink my sprightly wine:
Well I sup, and well I dine,
When I drink my frolic wine—
But I languish, lour and pine,
When I want my fragrant wine.
                    —ROBERT HERRICK

See also the COUPLET for a discussion of this form.

The BALADA is a dance song with an insistent refrain. A
CACCIA or CATCH is a longer ROUNDELAY—any simple lyric
that utilizes a refrain:

The Isle Is Full of Noises

What if, tomorrow, after your coffee,
after your Wheaties, while you're buttoning your clothes—
a dove descends and inspects your chimney?
    (What if it doesn't?)
        Expect nothing. Suppose.

What if, while putting your room in order,
after you've stashed every thing where it goes—
you see that your mirror's haloed in foxfire?
    (What if it isn't?)
        Expect nothing. Suppose.

What if, during your smoke on the parkbench,
after your cogitations, before your doze—
who should kiss you but a leftover virgin?
    (What if she doesn't?)
        Expect nothing. Suppose.

What if, suddenly, deep in a bookstore,
a ghost voice comes leap-frogging over the rows—
the voice says, "I love you." It's your father's.
    (What if it isn't?)
        Expect nothing. Suppose.

What if, one evening, watering your bean patch,
kite-caught, you quicken: you know what God knows—

the salt of your tears withers the sproutlings—
　　What if it doesn't?
　　Suppose. Suppose. Suppose.

　　　　　　　　　　　　　—SAM HUDSON

The CANSO, CANZO, or CANZONE is a song about beauty
and love, for example, "To His Coy Mistress" by Andrew
Marvell.

A CHANTEY is a work song, particularly a work song sung
by sailors. See "Hornpipepithalamium" later in this section.
The DITHYRAMB is a wild song honoring revelry:

Jolly Rutterkin

Rutterkin has come to town—
　　Hey! jolly rutter, hey!
Without a cloak nor coat nor gown,
But a good green hood upon his crown
　　Like a hoyden rutter!

Rutterkin has no English—
　　Hey! jolly rutter, hey!
His tongue runs on like butterfish
Smeared with grease upon his dish
　　Like a hoyden rutter!

Kiss Rutterkin and change your luck—
　　Hey! jolly rutter, hey!
He takes his ale down at a suck
Till he be wiser than a duck
　　Like a hoyden rutter!

When Rutterkin gets up from board—
　　Hey! jolly rutter, hey!
He'll piss a gallon in a gourd,
Then take the lasses like a lord
　　Like a hoyden Rutter!

　　　　　　　　　　　　　—ANONYMOUS

A DITTY is any simple lyric meant to be sung.
The ELEGY—one of the two major forms of OCCASION-

ALS—is a serious lyric meditation, often on the subject of death; see William Cullen Bryant's "Thanatopsis" and the section on ELEGIACS. Other, more intense lyrics of lamentation (see the LAMENT) are the CORONACH, DIRGE, MONODY, and THRENODY:

A Lie-Awake Dirge

This very night, this very night,
　　Every night and all,
Fire and sleet and candle-light,
　　And Christ receive your soul.

When you from hence away are passed,
　　Every night and all,
To Stony Moor you come at last,
　　And Christ receive your soul.

If ever you gave hose and shoes,
　　Every night and all,
Sit ye down, put them to use,
　　And Christ receive your soul.

If hose and shoes you gave to none,
　　Every night and all,
The winds shall prick you to the bare bone,
　　And Christ receive your soul.

When from the Bridge of Dread you pass,
　　Every night and all,
To Purgatory's fire you come at last,
　　And Christ receive your soul.

If ever you gave meat or drink,
　　Every night and all,
The fire shall never make you shrink,
　　And Christ receive your soul.

If meat or drink you gave to none,
　　Every night and all,
The fire will burn you to the bare bone,
　　And Christ receive your soul.

This very night, this very night,
    Every night and all,
Fire and sleet and candle-light,
    And Christ receive your soul.
                    —ANONYMOUS

The EPITHALAMION or EPITHALAMIUM is a marital elegy or wedding song, a form of OCCASIONALS. Originally it was written in three movements or strophes. The first part was to be sung at the chamber door of the bridegroom and bride. It was congratulatory in nature—it urged the newlyweds to lusty combat and was designed to muffle the sounds of that encounter. The second strophe was intended to refresh the combatants and urge them to fresh efforts during the night. The third movement, sung in the morning, congratulated the couple on their performances, urged a truce until the next evening, and instructed them in their domestic and marital duties. A meditative lyric on the same subject is called a PROTHALAMION or PROTHALAMIUM.

Hornpipepithalamium

The sea blows high and the wind blows cold,
    The *Hornet* sails out to sting.
We bellbottom boys are bully and bold,
Young at the moment but growing old,
And it's no damn good that I bought Jean a ring,
    I bought pretty Jean a ring.

The Gunner's Apprentice is cute as a pin,
    The Yeoman can really swing.
Those almond-eyed girls all know how to sin
To make your eyes swivel and your head spin—
But *I* had to go buy Jeannie a ring,
    A yellowish diamond ring.

Davy Jones flirts with the mermaids below.
    Down there where Neptune is king
The seacows come swimming along in a row
With nothing more on than a green weed bow

While the drowned sailors gather around in a ring
    And dance till the fathoms ring,

For each wooed a maiden of iron and steel,
    Then took her out for a fling.
She had a pert hull and a lovely keel,
But one day she just wouldn't answer her wheel—
I wonder if Jeannie's still wearing her ring,
    That beautiful bargain ring.

The wind blows cold, the sea blows high;
    I stand here trying to sing,
But the salt spray rises to spit in my eye
Till I'm ready to kill and fit to die
While Jeannie sits home and stares at her ring,
    For I gave sweet Jean my ring.

                                    —WESLI COURT

The LAMENT is a song of complaint.

Three Mourning Songs and an Oath

i.
Merry it is while summer lasts
    With wildfowls' song;
But now there nears the windy blast
    And weather strong.
O! O! but this night is long!
And I, weighed down with heavy wrong,
    Sorrow and sigh and fast.

ii.
Fowls in the firth,
    The fishes in the flood—
    And I may wax mad!
Much sorrow I walk with,
    For I am of bone and blood.

iii.
The life of this world
    Is ruled with wind,
Weeping, darkness,

> And with pain;
> With wind we bloom,
> With wind we decrease,
> With weeping we come,
> With weeping we pass.
> With pain we begin,
> With pain we end,
> With dread we dwell,
> With dread we wend.

iv.

> I've been a forester many a long day;
> My locks are white with hoar.
> I'll hang up my horn by the green wood spray—
> Forester I will be no more.
> The while that I may my bow bend
> I shall wed no wife.
> I shall build me a bower at the wood's end,
> And there I will lead my life.

> —ANONYMOUS

The BLUES is a modern form of complaint—see BLUES STANZA.

The LAY is a short narrative song—not to be confused with the French LAI, which is a set form. An example would be "La Belle Dame Sans Merci" by John Keats.

The MADRIGAL is a lyric concerning love, meant to be sung.

Mulidor's Madrigal

> Dildido, dildido,
> O love, O love,
> I feel thy rage rumble below and above!

> In summer time I saw a face,
> *Trop belle pour moi, helas, helas!*
> Like to a stoned horse was her pace:
> Was ever young man so dismayed?
> Her eyes, like wax torches, did make me afraid:
> *Trop belle pour moi, voila mon trepas*

Thy beauty, my love, exceedeth supposes;
Thy hair is a nettle for the nicest roses.
  Mon Dieu, aide moi!
That I with the primrose of my fresh wit
May tumble her tyranny under my feet:
  He! donc je serai un jeune roi.
Trop belle pour moi, helas, helas!
Trop belle pour moi, voila mon trepas.
—ROBERT GREENE

There are two strict forms of the madrigal listed under its own heading. The MADSONG, too, is listed separately under MADSONG STANZA. NONSENSE VERSE is what the name implies. "Jabberwocky" by Lewis Carroll is a MOCK BALLAD—see SATIRICS.

A NURSERY RHYME is a song for children(?):

The Lady and the Swine

There was a lady loved a swine,
  "Honey!" said she;
"Pig-hog, wilt thou be mine?"
  Hunc, said he.

"I'll build thee a silver sty,
  Honey," said she;
"And in it thou shalt lie."
  Hunc, said he.

"Pinned with a silver pin,
  Honey," said she;
"That thou may'st go out and in."
  Hunc, said he.

"Wilt thou have me now,
  Honey?" said she;
"Speak, or my heart will break!"
  Hunc, hunc, hunc! said he.
—ANONYMOUS

The ODE is one of the two major *forms* of the minor *genre* of OCCASIONALS, as well as of lyrics, the other being the EL-

EGY. The PAEAN is a song of praise to the gods; a PANEGYRIC or ENCOMIUM praises men. The PASTORAL and similar forms are treated in the section on BUCOLICS. For the REVEILLE, look in this section under ALBA and AUBADE. For the RIDDLE, see DIDACTICS. The ROMANCE (or METRICAL ROMANCE, to distinguish it from prose) is a verse tale whose subject matter concerns chivalry or honor.

A ROUNDELAY is any simple lyric that utilizes a refrain. A set form was invented by John Dryden, and it is to be found listed separately. See also the French ROUNDELET.

Song from Aella

O! sing unto my roundelay;
  O! drop the briny tear with me;
Dance no more at holiday;
  Like a running river be.
    My love is dead,
    Gone to his death-bed
    All under the willow tree.

Black his hair as the winter night,
  White his skin as the summer snow,
Red his face as the morning light;
  Cold he lies in the grave below.
    My love is dead,
    Gone to his death-bed
    All under the willow tree.

Sweet his tongue as the throstle's note,
  Quick in dance as thought can be,
Deft his tabor, cudgel stout;
  O! he lies by the willow-tree.
    My love is dead,
    Gone to his death-bed
    All under the willow tree.

See! the white moon shines on high,
  Whiter is my true love's shroud,
Whiter than the morning sky,
  Whiter than the evening cloud.

My love is dead,
Gone to his death-bed
All under the willow tree.

Come, with acorn-cup and thorn,
 Drain my own heart's blood away;
Life and all its good I scorn,
 Dance by night, or feast by day.
 My love is dead,
 Gone to his death-bed
 All under the willow tree.
 —THOMAS CHATTERTON

A RUNE is an Anglo-Saxon INCANTATION—see "The Mystery" by Amergin. Finally, coming full circle, the SERENADE is like the aubade, except that its setting is the evening. "She Walks in Beauty" by George Gordon, Lord Byron, is a standard example.

MADRIGAL

Italian and English. The Italian madrigal is written in lines of either seven or eleven syllables and is comprised of two or three triplets, followed by one or two rhyming couplets. There is no set rhyme scheme for the triplets, but if the poem were written in TERZA RIMA it might look like this:

lines	rhymes	lines	rhymes	lines	rhymes	lines	rhymes
1.	a	4.	b	7.	c	10.	d
2.	b	5.	c	8.	d	11.	d
3.	a	6.	b	9.	c	12.	a
						13.	a

The strict English madrigal was an accentual-syllabic invention of Geoffrey Chaucer. Written in iambic pentameter measures, it is comprised of three stanzas, the first of which is a *triplet*. *All* the lines of this triplet, which is used as though it were a texte, are refrains. The second stanza is a QUATRAIN. Lines six (6) and seven (7) of the poem (three and four of the quatrain) are lines one (1) and two (2) of the trip-

let repeated. The third stanza is a SESTET, the last three lines
of which are the first triplet repeated. The rhyme scheme of
the poem is $AB^1B^2abAB^1abbAB^1B^2$, which is easier to see in
a schematic diagram:

lines	rhymes, refrains	lines	rhymes, refrains	lines	rhymes, refrains
1.	A —refrain	4.	a	8.	a
2.	B¹—refrain	5.	b	9.	b
3.	B²—refrain	6.	A —refrain	10.	b
		7.	B¹—refrain	11.	A —refrain
				12.	B¹—refrain
				13.	B²—refrain

Chaucer wrote, in "Merciless Beauty," a series of three such
madrigals:

Merciless Beauty

i. *Captivity*
Your two eyes will slay me suddenly—
The beauty of them I may not sustain,
They pierce and wound my heart with blade so keen.

Only your word will bind up instantly
My heart's hurt while still the wound is green;
　　Your two eyes will slay me suddenly—
　　The beauty of them I may not sustain.

Upon my troth, I tell you faithfully
That of my life and death you are the queen,
For with my death the truth shall soon be seen—
　　Your two eyes will slay me suddenly—
　　The beauty of them I may not sustain,
　　They pierce and wound my heart with blade so keen.

ii. *Rejection*
Your beauty has from your heart so chased
Pity, it is useless to complain,
For Danger winds your mercy in his chain.

Though I am guiltless, my death you have purchased—
I tell you true, I do not need to feign;

Your beauty has from your heart so chased
Pity, it is useless to complain.

Alas! that nature has in you compassed
Such great beauty, no man may attain
To mercy, though he starve because of pain.
　　Your beauty has from your heart so chased
　　Pity, it is useless to complain,
　　For Danger winds your mercy in his chain.

iii. *Escape*
Since I from Love have thus escaped so fat,
I never plan to be back in prison lean;
Since I am free, Love isn't worth a bean.

He may reply, answer this or that—
I snap my fingers, speak just what I mean.
　　Since I from Love have thus escaped so fat,
　　I never plan to be back in prison lean.

Love has struck my name clear off his slate,
And from my ledger he is stricken clean
Forevermore—there is no in-between.
　　Since I from Love have thus escaped so fat,
　　I never plan to be back in prison lean.
　　Since I am free, Love isn't worth a bean.
　　　　　　　　　　　—GEOFFREY CHAUCER

For freer forms, see the section concerning LYRICS.

MADSONG, MADSONG STANZA—*see* LIMERICK,
　LYRICS.

MASK, MASQUE—*see* DRAMATICS.

MIRACLE PLAY—*see* DRAMATICS.

MONDO—*see* FORENSICS, KATAUTA.

MONK'S TALE STANZA—*see* HUITAIN.

MONODY
An ELEGY for the dead delivered by a single person.

MONOLOGUE—*see* DRAMATICS.

MORALITY PLAY—*see* DRAMATICS.

MORNINGSONG
A formal lyric prayer to be sung at dawn. See LITURGICS.

MOTE
Spanish. A mote is any poem of one or two lines, containing a complete statement or thought. The mote can serve as a texte to be glossed in verse, as in the GLOSE.

There are any number of set, single-line forms that might serve as motes, including the ALEXANDRINE, SEPTENARY, and the CLASSICAL HEROIC LINE. See also the COUPLET.

MOTTO—see MOTE, POSIE.

MYSTERY PLAY—*see* DRAMATICS.

NARRATIVES
Narratives is one of the three major subgenres of poetry. The four basic elements of narration are *character, plot, atmosphere,* and *theme.*

Theme is the thread of ideas that underlies the story. All narrative elements support the theme, which must be distinguished from the *subject.* The subject of a narrative can be expressed in a word or phrase, but the theme is *always* expressible only in a complete sentence (see DIDACTICS).

Character has to do with the personal characteristics of the persons in the narrative. These personal characteristics determine the actions and reactions of the persons in the story. The only person absolutely necessary is the *protagonist* (the main character). A narrative can have a multiple protagonist (a group or village, for instance), though normally one person will represent such a composite protagonist. A protagonist has two qualities: a desire—to *be,* to *do,* or to *have* something—and a dominant personality trait, such as courage, generosity, or fervor. The protagonist's desire drives her or him toward an objective or *goal*. Attainment of the goal will be blocked by a logical *antagonist*. The antagonist can be another person in opposition, a situation (being lost in a blizzard), a force (society), or oneself (an inner conflict). The opposition of protagonist versus antagonist leads to conflict, which is essential to the *dramatic situation* (to be distinguished from the *dramatic viewpoint*).

Plot concerns the actions and events that take place in the narrative and the *resolution* of the conflict between protagonist and antagonist. Just as theme is the thread of thought that binds all elements of the narrative together, plot can be defined as the thread of actions and events that carries the story and serves to exemplify the theme.

Atmosphere is the mood of the narrative, and mood is created by means of *setting* (locale and surroundings in which the narrative takes place), *attitude* (of the narrator and of the characters in the narrative), and *descriptions* (the sensory level).

Structure of the Narrative. Narratives can emphasize any one of the four basic elements or any combination of the four. Furthermore, the author tells the story from a particular narrative *viewpoint*. In reviewing this subject, I will break down *narrative voice,* covered earlier, into subcategories:

A. *Orientation.*

1. In the *author-oriented* narrative viewpoint, the author narrates the story.

2. In the *character-oriented* narrative viewpoint, a character in the story narrates.

    a. A major character (protagonist or antagonist).

    b. A minor character.

B. *Person.*

1. The story can be narrated in the *first person singular* (I saw what happened) or possibly first person plural (We saw what happened).

2. It could also be narrated in the *second person singular* or possibly second person plural (You saw what happened).

3. Finally, the story can be told in the *third person singular* (He, she, it saw what happened) or *plural* (they saw what happened).

C. *Angle.*

1. From the *single-angle*, only the actions of one character are followed; only what occurs in that character's presence is narrated.

2. From the *multiple-angle* (double, triple, etc.), what occurs in the presence of two or more characters is narrated.

3. From the *omnipresent angle*, the narrator has access to actions everywhere in the story.

D. *Access.*

1. The narrator might have only *objective access* to occurrences, being able to narrate only actions seen or heard.

2. The narrator might have *subjective access*, being able to narrate not only actions and words but the thoughts and emotions of characters as well.

As with all other elements, the narrator can blend any combination of orientation, person, access, and angle. The *omniscient viewpoint* is a combination of *author-oriented, third person,* and *omnipresent angle* narration with *subjective access.* In other words, the narrator knows all about everything, internal and external, everywhere in the story and narrates it thus.

Complication. The complication story emphasizes *plot.* A model complication story is structured as follows:

Inciting moment. It begins at a crucial point in the narrative, often *in medias res,* "in the middle of things"; that is, in the center of the main action. Epics traditionally begin this way.

Exposition. The story then gives necessary background information and provides partial answers to the questions, who or what? where? when? and sometimes, why?

Body. The main part of the story is a series of *rising actions,* or increasingly stronger attempts on the part of the protagonist to achieve the goal. Each successive action culminates in a *crisis,* or critical moment, when protagonist and antagonist are pitted against one another. In each attempt, the protagonist either fails or only partially succeeds.

Climax. In time, the series of rising actions leads to an ultimate crisis, when protagonist and antagonist are pitted against one another in a final effort. At this point, the protagonist either overcomes the antagonist and achieves the goal, or the conflict is lost. The *black moment* is the point in the climax when things look darkest for the chances of the protagonist.

Denouement. In the winding-down of the story, all actions are resolved and the story is concluded.

Conclusion. The ending of the story is either *open* or *closed*—either all loose ends are tied up neatly, or the story ends ambiguously: the actions may have been resolved, but not necessarily the attitudes of the narrator, the author, or the reader. Many modern narratives are open-ended; they are *inclusive*. Traditional narratives are often closed; they are *exclusive*.

Often a complication story will involve a subplot or secondary story line that runs parallel to the main story line—particularly in longer narratives. The subplot, generally, involves secondary characters of the narrative, and the actions of these characters serve to *complicate* or impede the main action. Often the protagonist will have to deal with the subplot's impediments before he or she can go on to deal with the main conflict, hence the term "complication" for a narrative that emphasizes plot and action.

Narrative Forms. There are a number of narrative poems, the chief of which is the EPIC, a long *heroic* verse narrative. Another important long form is the ROMANCE—a long *lyric* verse narrative. The BALLAD (which, though often written in specific stanza forms, in fact has no particular set form) is a relatively short *lyric* verse narrative. The FABLIAU is a short story in verse; the LAY is a vignette in song form. An EPYLLION is a "little epic," originally composed in dactylic hexameter verse. The BEAST EPIC uses animals for its characters, like the FABLE, which is a didactic allegory. The CHANSON DE GESTE is a type of medieval French epic with marked lyric qualities. An EXEMPLUM is a brief verse narrative, anecdotal in nature, used to illustrate a particular didactic point.

A number of French poetic forms—such as from the BAL-LADE family, including the CHANT ROYAL (the longest of the forms)—have been traditionally used to tell stories, but in fact most poets choose nonce forms, and stories have been told in every prosody. There are examples of narrative poems throughout this volume.

Obviously, there is no room in a book such as this for examples of the longest of the forms, but we might mention some of the better-known works in English. The greatest English epic is generally conceded to be John Milton's *Paradise Lost*. The longest and most unreadable is Edmund Spenser's *The Faery Queen,* though this work is perhaps more an interminable romance than an epic.

America's most successful epic is Stephen Vincent Benet's *John Brown's Body,* which has long been overlooked as grand narrative. Perhaps the reason for this oversight is that it is the world's most readable epic, and moderns possibly suspect that the epic, as "high art," ought not to be readable. Benet's poem, which is about the Civil War, has been described as a "cinema epic" because the structure of the poem is episodic, flashing from one part of the conflict to another. Passages of adventure and action are mixed with exquisite lyric interludes and songs, the camera eye of the narrator zooming in for a closeup, then pulling back for long-range shots and exposition. The poem lends itself well to dramatic rendition, and it was performed on Broadway in 1953 in an adaptation by Charles Laughton. The performance was a hit, and it was recorded by Columbia Records the same year.

Critics have attempted to claim epical stature for Walt Whitman's *Song of Myself,* but the poet had more insight, as the title tells us: it is an egopoem, not a narrative one. To define such a work as an "epic" is to distort the form and tradition of narrative art. The poem is the longest confessional poem in the history of literature, but it is boring in the end because Whitman did not have a lyric ear. The work sags with prolixity, seldom if ever rising to the level of song. Neither does it tell a story, not even the autobiography of the author; there is thus nothing to support the interest of the reader.

Similarly, Ezra Pound's *Cantos* cannot be called an epic because it, too, is largely confessional in nature. Furthermore, no one has been able to identify a central character (other than the narrator), plot, or theme that unifies the "actions" of the poem. Pound, too, was much closer to the mark when he titled it as he did: the poem is a series of cantos that lead nowhere specific. No resolution takes place, there is no discernible beginning, middle, or end; therefore, it is a set, not even a sequence, although one that contains some brilliant writing. The work might better be thought of as the collected, later poems of Ezra Pound.

William Carlos Williams' *Paterson* comes closer to the model of an epic than Pound's *Cantos,* but it is even more episodic and jumpy than Benet's *John Brown's Body.* Nevertheless, it is readable and in parts—even, perhaps, overall— narrative. An interesting—truly interesting—poem built on the model of Williams' piece is Charlie Davis' *And So the Irish Built a Church.* H. D. (Hilda Doolittle) wrote a long narrative, *Helen in Egypt,* and Edwin Arlington Robinson wrote several, but these are more on the order of novellas in verse than of epics. Conrad Aiken, too, has written both long, beautifully lyrical narrative poems and sequences of poems that function as narration but do not try the short attention-spans of contemporary readers.

NASHER—*see* SATIRICS.

NIGHTSONG
A formal lyric prayer to be sung at midnight. See LITURGICS.

NOH PLAY—*see* DRAMATICS.
NONSENSE VERSE—*see* LYRICS.
NURSERY RHYME—*see* LYRICS.

OBSEQUY

A formal lyric mourning the dead; a funeral song. See EPI-
CEDIUM, MONODY; also, DIRGE, ELEGY, OCCASIONALS.

OCCASIONALS

A minor subgenre of poetry. I have already spoken of the
ODE and the ELEGY, the two major forms of occasionals, in
the sections on ELEGIACS, LYRICS, and elsewhere.

Wordsworth's "Ode: On the Intimations of Immortality"
is an IRREGULAR ODE. Keats' "To Autumn" is an ENGLISH ODE,
his invention. Milton's "On the Morning of Christ's Nativ-
ity" is a HOMOSTROPHIC ODE; though it uses two stanza
forms, those in each of the two movements are alike. These
poems can be found in *Poetry: An Introduction* (op. cit.) and
elsewhere. The PINDARIC ODE is described in the section on
the ODE.

There are various other kinds of occasional poems de-
scribed elsewhere in these pages, such as the EPITHALAMION
or wedding celebration, the PROTHALAMION, and so forth.

OCTAVE

A STANZA consisting of eight lines. It can be written in any
meter, rhymed or unrhymed. Lines can be of any length.
Rhymes, if any, can be random or regular.

The ITALIAN OCTAVE is written in iambic pentameter lines,
and it rhymes *abbaabba* (see the ITALIAN SONNET). The SI-
CILIAN OCTAVE is also accentual-syllabic. It is a STANZA of
iambic pentameter lines turning on two rhymes. It can also
be a complete poem. The diagram of the Sicilian octave
looks like this:

lines	meters and rhymes
1.	xx xx xx xx xa
2.	xx xx xx xx xb

lines	meters and rhymes
3.	x́x x́x x́x x́x x́a
4.	x́x x́x x́x x́x x́b
5.	x́x x́x x́x x́x x́a
6.	x́x x́x x́x x́x x́b
7.	x́x x́x x́x x́x x́a
8.	x́x x́x x́x x́x x́b

The STRAMBOTTO is a Sicilian octave in hendecasyllabic lines. For an excellent octave poem, see James Wright's "Song for the Middle of the Night" in *Strong Measures* (op. cit.). For closely related forms, see OTTAVA RIMA, the Sicilian SESTET, and the second ending of the Italian SONNET. See also the section on HEROICS.

ODE

There are three more or less strict forms of the ode. The first is the PINDARIC ODE, which is of Greek origin. It is usually written in accentual-syllabic verse. The stanza pattern, rhyme scheme, and line-lengths are determined by the poet. The poem is divided into three *movements,* the first of which is called the *strophe.* The second movement, called the *antistrophe,* is identical to the first. The third and last movement of the poem is called the *stand* or *epode.* Its form is strict also, but entirely different from that of the first two movements.

Derived from the classical tragedy, the content of the strophe is an argument in favor of a point-of-view spoken by a chorus on one side of the stage. To consider the opposite view, the chorus travels to the other side of the stage and voices its concerns. In the epode, the chorus moves to center stage to deliver its conclusion upon the matter under consideration. This internal form is still the tradition. See DRAMATICS.

The ENGLISH ODE (or Keatsian ode) is accentual-syllabic. It

consists of three, ten-line iambic pentameter stanzas. Stanza one rhymes *ababcdecde;* stanzas two and three have the same scheme but their own rhymes. This pattern was derived by combining elements of the English and Italian SONNET forms: a Sicilian QUATRAIN from the English sonnet (*abab*) is attached to an Italian SESTET (*cdecde*). Though John Keats is given credit for inventing this form, he did not follow it exactly in any of his famous odes. The "Ode on Melancholy" comes closest, but there is a rhyme variant in stanza three. "To Autumn" has eleven-line stanzas. This poem adheres to the form, though it begins with an *epigraph:*

The Man Hunter

"But we were born of risen apes, not fallen angels, and the apes were armed killers besides. And so what shall we wonder at? . . . The miracle of man is not how far he has sunk but how magnificently he has risen. We are known among the stars by our poems, not our corpses."—Robert Ardrey in *African Genesis.*

When I saw, spinning webs of sense and dust,
   The heart-shaped spider of the womb's demands,
I raised myself upright upon the crust
   Of earth and issued it my first commands:
"Give me what I may take before the glass
   Of time is empty as a brain's white bowl
     Where slugs drink, where the mosses gorge and green."
I walked out of the forest, across the grass—
   It withered underneath my callous sole,
     For I could not forget what I had seen.

I saw the scarab in the turning earth
   Spinning murders from its golden shell;
I saw the rooting beast probing death,
   But death must root if it would hope to dwell.
Therefore I walked the trench of lambs and ewes
   With winter's humour snowing in my bones,
     And in my web of veins the scratching, dumb,
Dry tongue of the beast feeding on my dews.
   Then, when at last I lay down in these stones,
     I knew that more of us would one day come.

And you have come to find yourself in me
   Here where I lie, a skull transformed to stone.
My sightless eyes look out at you and see
   That under the eons we are still alone—
But we are millions now who were a few
   To forsake the forest and face time with a rock,
     A naked rock held in a naked hand.
We face the ages still, and we bestrew
   This cairn of stars with the remnants of our stock:
     A jawbone here and there wearing to sand.

—WESLI COURT

The HOMOSTROPHIC ODE (or Horatian Ode) consists of any number of *formal* nonce stanzas:

An Ode to Himself

   Where dost thou careless lie,
     Buried in ease and sloth?
   Knowledge that sleeps doth die;
   And this security,
     It is the common moth
That eats on wits and arts, and oft destroys them both:

   Are all the Aonian springs
     Dried up? Lies Thespia waste?
   Doth Clarius' harp want strings,
   That not a nymph now sings?
     Or droop they as disgraced,
To see their seats and bowers by chattering 'pies defaced?

   If hence thy silence be,
     As 'tis too just a cause,
   Let this thought quicken thee:
   Minds that are great and free
     Should not on fortune pause;
'Tis crown enough to virtue still, her own applause.

   What though the greedy fry
     Be taken with false baits
   Of worded balladry,
   And think it poesy?

They die with their conceits,
And only piteous scorn upon their folly waits.

Then take in hand thy lyre;
    Strike in thy proper strain;
With Japhet's line aspire
Sol's chariot for new fire
    To give the world again;
Who aided him will thee, the issue of Jove's brain.

And, since our dainty age
    Cannot endure reproof,
Make not thyself a page
To that strumpet the stage;
    But sing high and aloof,
Safe from the wolf's black jaw, and the dull ass's hoof.

—BEN JONSON

A fourth type, the Cowleyan or IRREGULAR ODE, is a loose form. It can be described simply as a serious lyric that commemorates an event. It, too, is a nonce form. An example is Wordsworth's "Ode: Intimations of Immortality from Recollections of Early Childhood," widely available in anthologies. In this case, the poem is variable, normative accentual-syllabics, strophic, and randomly rhymed.

The French, syllabic RONSARDIAN ODE is, strictly speaking, a STANZA form. Such an ode can be of any length, provided each stanza is nine lines long, rhymes *ababccddc,* and varies its line-lengths between decasyllabics and tetrasyllabics in a specific order. The *last* line is an octosyllabic line:

lines	syllables and rhymes
1.	x x x x x x x x x a
2.	x x x b
3.	x x x x x x x x x a
4.	x x x b
5.	x x x x x x x x x c
6.	x x x x x x x x x c
7.	x x x d

lines	*syllables and rhymes*
8.	x x x d
9.	x x x x x x x c

See also LYRICS and OCCASIONALS.

OTTAVA RIMA

An Italian STANZA pattern. It can also be a complete poem. It is an OCTAVE stanza in iambic pentameter lines, rhyming *abababcc*. Essentially, ottava rima is a Sicilian SESTET expanded by the addition of a HEROIC COUPLET. For contemporary examples, see Gjertrude Schnackenberg's "How Did It Seem to Sylvia?" (a one-stanza poem) and David R. Slavitt's longer, "Another Letter to Lord Byron," in *Strong Measures* (op. cit.).

For related forms, see the Italian OCTAVE and the Sicilian OCTAVE in the section on the SONETTO RISPETTO.

PAEAN—*see* LYRICS.

PALINODE

A Greek and Italian form. A palinode is a lyric "song of retraction" for a derogatory statement that has been made. A set form consists of *two strophes* and *two antistrophes*. These are nonce forms but, as in the ODE, the poet sets a pattern that must be adhered to throughout the poem.

The pattern of the first strophe is mirrored in the last antistrophe; the pattern of the second strophe is mirrored in the first antistrophe: strophe *A*, strophe *B*, antistrophe *B*, antistrophe *A*, in that order. The two strophes might be the statement, and the two antistrophes might be the retraction. Technically, the two (differing) strophes are called the *ode*, and the two (differing) antistrophes are the *palinode* proper.

Palinode

I.
When I was young and light of heart
I made sad songs with easy art:
Now I am sad, and no more young,
My sorrow cannot find a tongue.

II.
Pray, Muses, since I may not sing
Of Death or any grievous thing,
Teach me some joyous strain, that I
May mock my youth's hypocrisy!
　　　—THOMAS BAILEY ALDRICH

PANEGYRIC—*see* ENCOMIUM, LYRICS.

PANTOUM
A Malayan form. Accentual-syllabic. Lines can be of any
single length in any particular meter. A pantoum consists of
an indefinite number of *quatrain stanzas* with particular re-
strictions: lines two and four of each stanza, *in their entirety,*
are repetons—they become lines one and three of the follow-
ing stanza, and so on. The rhyme scheme is interlocking.

　　The poem can be ended in one of two ways: either in a
QUATRAIN whose repetons are lines one and three of the *first*
stanza *in reversed order,* or in a repeton couplet consisting of
lines one and three of the first stanza *in reversed order.* The
pattern for a four-stanza poem would be:

lines	rhymes and repetons	lines	rhymes and repetons
1.	A^1	9.	C^1
2.	B^1	10.	D^1
3.	A^2	11.	C^2
4.	B^2	12.	D^2
5.	B^1	13.	Z^1 or A^2
6.	C^1	14.	A^2 or A^1
7.	B^2	15.	Z^2
8.	C^2	16.	A^1

The Eunuch Cat

She went to work until she grew too old,
    Came home at night to feed the eunuch cat
That kept the mat warm and its eyeballs cold.
    She walked, but ran to wrinkles, then to fat,

    Came home at night to feed the eunuch cat,
Then went to bed, slept dreamlessly till eight,
    And waked. She ran to wrinkles, then to fat.
She fixed her supper, snacked till it was late,

Then went to bed, slept dreamlessly till eight—
    Must I go on? She'll feed the cat no more.
She fixed her supper, snacked till it was late,
    Then died at dawn, just halfway through a snore.

    Must I go on?—she'll feed the cat no more
To keep the mat warm and its eyeballs cold.
    She died at dawn, just halfway through a snore;
She went to work until she grew too old.

                              —WESLI COURT

For other examples of contemporary pantoums, see "A
Pantoum for Morning" by Claire McAllister in *Poetry* (op.
cit.); see also several pantoums, including variations, by John
Ashbery, Donald Justice, Thomas Lux, Peter Meinke, and
Pamela Stewart in *Strong Measures* (op. cit.).

PASSION PLAY—*see* DRAMATICS.

PASTORAL, PASTORALE—*see* BUCOLICS.

PASTORAL ELEGY, PASTORAL ODE—*see* BUCOLICS,
    LYRICS, OCCASIONALS.

PASTOURELLE—*see* BUCOLICS *and* NARRATIVES.

PETRARCHAN SONNET—*see* ITALIAN SONNET.

PICTURE POEM—*see* SPATIALS.

PINDARIC ODE—*see* OCCASIONALS *and* ODE.

PLAMPEDE—*see* INTERLUDE.

POSIE

Single verse or couplet of an epigrammatic or aphoristic nature. See EPIGRAM, MOTE, MOTTO.

POULTER'S MEASURE

English. Accentual-syllabic. Rhymed. A COUPLET that alternates the ALEXANDRINE (see also SPENSERIAN STANZA) with the SEPTENARY or FOURTEENER. There can be any number of couplets in a stanza or poem.

The alexandrine is a *line* of iambic hexameter verse:

xx xx xx xx xx xx.

The fourteener was, in Latin verse, a *line* consisting of seven metrical feet. In English verse, the line contains fourteen syllables arranged in iambics, with a caesura appearing somewhere in the center of the line (after the third foot):

xx xx xx xx · xx xx xx.

A schematic of one couplet of Poulter's measure looks like this:

lines	meters, caesurae, and rhymes
1.	xx xx xx xx xx xa
2.	xx xx xx · xx xx xx xa

This next poem is written in fourteeners (each two lines equals one fourteener):

To Old Nobodaddy

Why art thou silent and invisible,
    Father of Jealousy?
Why dost thou hide thyself in clouds
    From every searching eye?
Why darkness and obscurity
    In all thy words and laws,—

That none dare eat the fruit but from
   The wily serpent's jaws?
Or is it because secrecy
   Gains feminine applause?
       —WILLIAM BLAKE

PRIMER COUPLET—*see* DIDACTICS.

PROSE POEM

If a poem is not written in verse—in a metrical prosody—
then it is written in prose. Usually the lines are determined
by line-phrasing—that is, lines are phrases or some other
unit of grammar. An example is Christopher Smart's "Of
the Spiritual Musick," to be found elsewhere in these pages.

Sometimes prose poems are built on a particular schema,
as for instance in "A Portrait of the Day" by Bill Sloan in
Alberta Turner's *Poets Teaching* (op. cit.), which is based on
the schema *epanodis*. A discussion accompanies the poem.

This next poem was composed in the prose prosody first
used in English by Ezra Pound in his translation of the *Shih-
ching* (Cambridge, 1954), notably in "Book I. Chou and the
South," nos. II, IV, and VI. Certain features of this prosody
include lines of uneven length, some of which are repeated
incrementally, true rhyme occasionally but consonance usu-
ally, and repetition and echo. The effect of this prosody is to
make prose as lyrical a vehicle for poetry as is traditional
(since Chaucer) accentual-syllabic prosody:

Dawn Song
". . . *world of the first rose, and the first lark's song.*"—*Margaret Mead*

I am the first to know dawn for the dawn—
It breaks across my mind as across the eyes
Of the beast I was, of the beasts from whom I come,
And the swift sun slows, and I know it for the sun
In the world of the first rose, and the first lark's song.

I am the first to see the sharp sun dawn,
Breaking across my terror and my surprise;
To know that I am the beast who knows his name:
Beast of the Sun, beast of the spinning sun
Of the world of the first rose, and the first lark's song.

I am the first to see stone for a stone,
To heft it in my hand, to feel its weight
and know what it may do to the brittle bone
Of the beasts of the sun, in the morning of the sun,
In the world of the first rose, and the first lark's song.

I see, and my sight is hard, hard as the stone
Held in my hand, and this stone will be my fate.
The beast is my brother—beast is his only name.
He is the child of dust. I am stone's son,
Born of the first rose, and the first lark's song.

—WESLI COURT

NASHERS, named after their inventor Ogden Nash, are couplets usually composed of long lines of flat prose with humorous, often multisyllabic endings utilizing wrenched rhymes. Nashers are often used satirically. For another satiric form built on an opposite prosody, see SKELTONICS in the section concerned with SATIRICS. See also the CATALOG.

PROTHALAMION, PROTHALAMIUM—*see* LYRICS, OCCASIONALS.

QASIDA—*see* COUPLET.

QUATORZAIN—*see* BREF DOUBLE.

QUATRAIN

A stanza or poem consisting of four lines. It can be written in any meter and line-length, rhymed or unrhymed. This poem uses analyzed rhyme:

Winter

The wind keens on the bare hill;
The ford is froar, and the lake

Is hoar-crusted. A man's ilk
Might stand on a single stalk.

Comber after comber comes
To cover the shore. The gale
Hovers over the hill: owls
Crying. One cannot stand tall.

The bed of the fish is cold
In the ice where they shelter.
Reeds are bearded; the stag, starved.
Trees bow in the early dusk.

Snow falls, and the earth is pale.
Warriors sit near their fires.
The lake is a dim defile:
No warmth is in its color.

Snow falls; the hoarfrost is white;
The shield is idle upon
The old man's shoulder. The wind
Freezes the grass with its whine.

Snow falls on top of the ice.
Wind sweeps the crest of the trees
Standing close. On his shoulder
The brave fighter's fine shield shines.

—ANONYMOUS

The ENVELOPE STANZA is a quatrain that rhymes *abba*. The so-called IN MEMORIAM STANZA is an iambic tetrameter envelope stanza. The REDONDILLA, a Spanish form of the envelope stanza, is an octosyllabic (in English measures, iambic tetrameter) quatrain, rhyming *abba, abab,* or *aabb*.

The ITALIAN QUATRAIN is an envelope stanza written in iambic pentameter measures:

lines	*meters and rhymes*
1.	xx xx xx xx xa
2.	xx xx xx xx xb

lines	meters and rhymes
3.	x́x x́x x́x x́x x́b
4.	x́x x́x x́x x́x x̄a

Doubled, it becomes the ITALIAN OCTAVE, which is utilized in the Italian SONNET. The Italian quatrain is a form of HEROIC STANZA.

The Sicilian QUATRAIN is also a set form of the HEROIC STANZA and is the pattern for the quatrain of the English SONNET. It is the same as the Italian octave, except that it rhymes *abab*. Doubled, it becomes the Sicilian OCTAVE.

There are examples of quatrain forms throughout these pages, including poems by William Blake and Emily Dickinson, both of whom used them almost exclusively. See also *Strong Measures* (op. cit.) for examples of the various kinds of quatrains.

For other set forms and uses of the quatrain see the sections on AE FREISLIGHE, ALCAICS, AWDL GYWYDD, BALLAD STANZA, BYR A THODDAID, CASBAIRDNE, COMMON MEASURE, DEIBHIDHE, the ENGLYNS, GWAWDODYN, KYRIELLE, PANTOUM, the RANNAIGHEACHTS, RIONNAIRD TRI-NARD, RISPETTO, ROUNDEL, RUBAI, SAPPHICS, SEADNA, SNEADHBHAIRDNE, and TODDAID.

QUINTET

A poem or stanza consisting of five lines. It can be in any meter and line-length, rhymed or unrhymed.

The SICILIAN QUINTET is written in iambic pentameter measures, and it rhymes *ababa*. The QUINTILLA, a Spanish form, is any *octosyllabic* (in English measures, iambic tetrameter) quintet rhyming *ababa, abbab, ababb, abaab, aabab,* or *aabba*. The ENVELOPE QUINTET rhymes *abcba* or *abbba*. The ENGLISH QUINTET is any quintet rhyming *ababb*. For examples of this form, see Robert Penn Warren's "Original Sin: A Short Story" and Randall Jarrell's "Eighth Air Force," both in *Strong Measures* (op. cit.).

The poems titled "Party Game" and "Poetry" earlier in these pages are written in quintet stanzas; the former is a QUINTILLA in normative accentual-syllabics, the latter, a NONCE FORM in quantitative syllabics broken into *verse paragraphs* as well as in quintet stanzas.

QUINTILLA—*see* QUINTET.

RANDAIGECHT CHETHARCHUBAID—*see*
 RANNAIGHEACHTS.

RANNAIGHEACHT BHEAG, GHAIRID, MHÓR—*see*
 RANNAIGHEACHTS.

RANNAIGHEACHTS *(ron-áyach)*

Irish. Syllabic. RANNAIGHEACHT GHAIRID (ron-áyach chár-rid) is a QUATRAIN STANZA. The first line is three syllables long, the rest are seven syllables in length. The quatrain single-rhymes *aaba*. Line three (3) cross-rhymes with line four (4).

In all the Irish forms in this section and elsewhere, the poem (not the stanza) ends with the same first syllable, word, or line with which it begins. The diagram for one stanza is thus:

lines	syllables and rhymes
1.	x x a
2.	x x x x x x a
3.	x x x x x x b
4.	x x *b* x *x* x a

In the following poem, the first line is a full line of seven syllables, not three, nor does the verse observe the circle-back convention:

Pocoangelini 10

Pocoangelini's feet
Were like two shovels. His beat
was down by the waterfront
where barges shunt and the neat

        gulls rudder
through the air; where the shudder
of engines among pilings
and piers makes silence flutter

        down the bay
like a flight of pigeons. Day
after day Poco, in big
shoes, would wiggle knobs on gray

        doors and swing
his billy. Then, one evening,
at his rattle a door flew
loosely wide. He stood staring

        on thresholds
of shadow into great folds
of darkness that hung down from
the rafters. Marigolds

        were the first
to bloom into his eyes. Worst
of all were the irises
rising from the thirst-

        raging well
of the warehouse. Then a bell's
sound, like snowdrop swans swimming,
came brimming his ears. It fell

        and gently
lay near his shoes: quite simply,
these had shrunk. He moved one pace
forward and was amazed—the

        ache vanished
as the monstrous garden washed
toward him like a rainbow
sea. Now fright drowned him; it dashed

        the door to
behind him. Poco's blue
figure hurtled down the street.
His feet throbbed and burned. He knew

they were blown
big as balloons again. Down
the walk he ran, stumbling, till
his shoes had swollen, had grown

back to their
former size. He would not stare
at so much gross beauty for
the fairest, the straightest pair

of strong feet
on the Force. Back on his beat
the gulls ruddered in the air,
wove rare threads through his retreat.
—L. T.

When the lines in this form end in *disyllables* instead of monosyllables, the form is called RANDAIGECHT CHETHAR-CHUBAID GARIT RECOMARCACH (ron-di-guech chey-er-hu-did gár-red ray-cúm-ar-cach).

RANNAIGHEACHT MHÓR (ron-áyach voor) is a QUATRAIN STANZA of heptasyllabic lines *consonating abab*. There are at least two cross-rhymes in each couplet of this form, and the final word of line three (3) rhymes with a word in the interior of line four (4). The internal rhyme in the first couplet can consonate rather than rhyme. In the second couplet, the rhymes must be exact. Two words alliterate in each line, the final word of line four (4) alliterating with the preceding stressed word. A simplified schematic would be:

lines	syllables, cross-rhymes, and consonations	
1.	x x x x b x ac	—lines 1 and 3, 2 and 4
2.	x x x a x x bc	*consonate*, they do not rhyme.
3.	x b x x x x ac	
4.	x x a x x x bc	

This poem observes all the conventions:

The Bard's Lament

Woodland's green wall is wilding,
Mild with the blackbird's preachment;

Cock and hen hover, a-wing,
Where I bring pen and parchment—

But the grey-hooded cuckoo
From his fastness mocks my mood.
Good grief! May God save those who
Would write well in the wildwood!
                    —ANONYMOUS

RANNAIGHEACHT BHEAG (ron-áyah viog) is the same, except the line endings are disyllabic. DEACHNADH MOR (dagnáw-moor) is also the same, except that lines one (1) and three (3) are octosyllabic, lines two (2) and four (4) are hexasyllabic, and all line endings are disyllabic words.

REDONDILLA—*see* QUATRAIN.

RENGA—*see* TANKA.

REVEILLE—*see* ALBA, AUBADE, LYRICS.

RHUPUNT *(rhée-pint)*
Welsh. Syllabic. A *line* of three, four, or five sections. Each section contains four syllables. All but the last section rhyme with each other. The last section carries the *main* rhyme from line to line (or from stanza to stanza, depending on how the lines are set up; that is, each section can be written on the page as a single line of verse).

In this pattern, each section is treated as one line, and each set of sections is treated as one stanza:

lines (or sections)	syllables and rhymes	
1.	x x x a	⎫
2.	x x x a	⎬ one line
3.	x x x a	⎪
4.	x x x B	⎭
5.	x x x c	⎫
6.	x x x c	⎬ one line
7.	x x x c	⎪
8.	x x x B	⎭

After two lines (sets of sections), the main rhyme can change:

A Winter Song

I have one song:
Stags are groaning,
Clouds are snowing—
Summer is gone.

Swiftly the sun
Settles beyond
The horizon,
Louring and wan.

The wild geese mourn
Down the grey storm;
Fallen is fern,
Tattered and brown.

The bird's feather
Is clogged with hoar;
This is my lore—
Summer is gone.
    —ANONYMOUS

TAWDDGYRCH CADWYNOG (tówdd-girch ca-dóy-nog) is, similarly, a *line* of three, four, or five sections. Each section contains four syllables. The rhyme scheme is *abbc*. Each section must rhyme with its corresponding section in at least one other line of verse. If desired, each section can be written as one *line* of verse. In the following schematic diagram, each section is treated as one line, and each set of sections is treated as one stanza:

lines (or sections)	syllables and rhymes	
1.	x x x a	
2.	x x x b	one line
3.	x x x b	
4.	x x x c	

lines (or sections)	syllables and rhymes	
5.	x x x a	
6.	x x x b	one line
7.	x x x b	
8.	x x x c	

After two lines (or sets of sections), the rhymes may change.

RIDDLE—*see* DIDACTICS.

RIMAS DISSOLUTAS
Originally French. Syllabic. Lines can be of any single length, and there can be any number of lines in a stanza. Lines within a stanza do not rhyme, but corresponding lines in subsequent stanzas *do* rhyme. The scheme for a quintet stanza of eight syllables is:

lines	syllables and rhymes	lines	syllables and rhymes
1.	x x x x x x x a	6.	x x x x x x x a
2.	x x x x x x x b	7.	x x x x x x x b
3.	x x x x x x x c	8.	x x x x x x x c
4.	x x x x x x x d	9.	x x x x x x x d
5.	x x x x x x x e	10.	x x x x x x x e

For an example of a contemporary poem in this form, see David Wagoner's "Staying Alive" in *Poetry* (op. cit.). This poem can also be found in *Strong Measures* (op. cit.), together with Sylvia Plath's "Black Root in Rainy Weather," Jon Anderson's "The Blue Animals," and several others.

RIME COUÉE
French. Syllabic. A SESTET STANZA made of two couplets of any single length and two shorter lines. One short line follows each couplet. The short lines rhyme with each other. A schematic diagram of rime couée in iambics would be:

lines	meters and rhymes
1.	x́x x́x x́x x́a
2.	x́x x́x x́x x́a
3.	x́x x́x x́b
4.	x́x x́x x́x x́c *or* x́a
5.	x́x x́x x́x x́c *or* x́a
6.	x́x x́x x́b

The Scottish BURNS STANZA or STANDARD HABBIE, a varia-
tion, rhymes $a^4a^4a^4b^2a^4b^2$. Following are two stanzas of a
Burns poem written in standard habbie:

*To a Mouse, on Turning Her Up in Her Nest with the
Plough, November, 1785*

Wee, sleekit, cow'rin, tim'rous beastie,
O, what a panic's in thy breastie!
Thou need na start awa sae hasty,
     Wi' bickering brattle!
I wad be laith to rin an' chase thee,
     Wi' murd'ring pattle!

I'm truly sorry man's dominion
Has broken Nature's social union,
An' justifies that ill opinion,
     Which makes thee startle
At me, thy poor, earth-born companion,
     An fellow-mortal!
        —ROBERT BURNS

RIME ROYAL

An English-Scottish form. Accentual-syllabic. A SEPTET
STANZA rhyming *ababbcc*. The lines are written in iambic
pentameter measures. For an example of rime royal, see
Chaucer's "Complaint to His Purse" in the section on the
BALLADE. Contemporary examples by Philip Dacey ("Jack,

Afterwards") and Al Lee ("Beside My Grandmother") can be found in *Strong Measures* (op. cit.).

RIONNAIRD TRI-NARD *(rún-ard tree-nard)*

Irish. Syllabic. A QUATRAIN STANZA of hexasyllabic lines with disyllabic endings. Lines two (2) and four (4) rhyme, and line three (3) consonates with them. There are two cross-rhymes in the second couplet, none in the first. There is alliteration in each line, and the last syllable of line one (1) alliterates with the first accented word of line two (2). There are two cross-rhymes in the second couplet, none in the first.

The poem, not the stanza, ends with the same first syllable, word, or line with which it begins:

lines	syllables and rhymes
1.	x x x x (x a)
2.	x x x x (x bc)
3.	x b x x (x c)—*line 3 consonates with lines 2 and 4*
4.	x x c x (x bc)

RISPETTO

An Italian form. Accentual-syllabic. Any complete poem consisting of two rhyming QUATRAINS, often rhyming *abab ccdd*. Many rispettos are written in iambic tetrameter measures, like the example here:

Two Epigrams

When I stand with the young bloods,
Then my fierce red blood is up;
When I sit with the greybeards,
I nod sagely in my cup.

Sad to see the sons of lore
Damned to the eternal fire
While these pigs, illiterate,
In God's glory corruscate.

—ANONYMOUS

If the rispetto is written in iambic pentameter measures, it can combine heroic forms—the Sicilian and Italian quatrains, or a Sicilian quatrain and two heroic couplets. It thus becomes a HEROIC RISPETTO.

For contemporary examples of the rispetto, see *Strong Measures* (op. cit.).

ROMANCE—*see* LYRICS *and* NARRATIVES.

RONDEAU

French. Syllabic or accentual-syllabic. The long lines of this form can be of any single length; the same is true for the short lines. The rondeau has fifteen lines divided into three stanzas: one QUINTET, one QUATRAIN, and one SESTET. The poem turns on two rhymes and is built on one refrain. The refrain consists of the first few words of the first line. In this schematic diagram, the refrain is represented by the letter *R:*

lines	rhymes and refrains	lines	rhymes and refrains
1.	. . . R a—*first line* contains *refrain*		
2.	a		
3.	b	10.	a
4.	b	11.	a
5.	a	12.	b
6.	a	13.	b
7.	a	14.	a
8.	b	15.	. . . R
9.	. . . R —*refrain*		

Rondeau

Help me to seek, for I lost it there,
And if that ye have found it, ye that be here,
And seek to convey it secretly,
Handle it soft and treat it tenderly,
Or else it will plain and then appear:

But rather restore it mannerly,
Since that I do ask it thus honestly:

For to lose it, it sitteth me too near.
    Help me to seek.

Alas, and is there no remedy?
But have I thus lost it wilfully?
Iwis it was a thing all too dear
To be bestowed and wist not where—
It was my heart, I pray you heartily,
    Help me to seek.
        —THOMAS WYATT

This next example was written by a Black American poet:

We Wear the Mask

We wear the mask that grins and lies,
It hides our cheeks and shades our eyes—
This debt we pay to human guile;
With torn and bleeding hearts we smile,
And mouth with myriad subtleties.

Why should the world be otherwise,
In counting all our tears and sighs?
Nay, let them only see us while
    We wear the mask.

We smile, but, O great Christ, our cries
To thee from tortured souls arise.
We sing, but oh the clay is vile
Beneath our feet, and long the mile;
But let the world dream otherwise,
    We wear the mask.
        —PAUL LAURENCE DUNBAR

For contemporary examples of the rondeau, see "Is It Well Lighted, Papa?" by James Bertram, "Rondeau After a Transatlantic Telephone Call" by Marilyn Hacker, and "Death of a Vermont Farm Woman" by Barbara Howes in *Strong Measures* (op. cit.).

RONDEAU REDOUBLED

The French rondeau redoublé consists of twenty-four lines of any single length, plus a twenty-fifth coda line—a refrain—made up of the first few words of the first line. These lines are divided into five QUATRAINS and one QUINTET. Stanza one rhymes *(RA¹)B¹A²B²;* each line in this first quatrain, which is a *texte,* is a refrain. Counting the internal refrain shown here as *R,* this texte contains five refrains.

The entire first line of the poem reappears as line eight (8), ending the second stanza; line two reappears as line twelve (12), ending the third stanza; line three reappears as line sixteen (16), ending the fourth stanza; line four reappears as line twenty (20), ending the fifth stanza; and the first few words of line one reappear as line twenty-five (25), ending the poem. The diagram:

lines		rhymes and refrains	lines	rhymes and refrains
t	1.	. . . R A¹—*line contains a refrain and is one.*		
e	2.	B¹—*refrain*		
x	3.	A²—*refrain*	13.	b
t	4.	B²—*refrain*	14.	a
e			15.	b
			16.	A²—*refrain*
	5.	b	17.	a
	6.	a	18.	b
	7.	b	19.	a
	8.	A¹—*refrain*	20.	B²—·*refrain*
	9.	a	21.	b
	10.	b	22.	a
	11.	a	23.	b
	12.	B¹—*refrain*	24.	a
			25.	. . . R —*refrain*

Jason Potter
(*from* Bordello)

Suddenly, nothing was left of all those
years we'd spent together in the same house,
under that old mansard that bent and rose
above us, gracefully guarding. The spruce

in the dooryard spired out of the grass
like a steeple, pulling us taut as bows—
both generations. But age is a noose:
suddenly, nothing was left of all those

mornings and nights. I, Jason Potter, chose
to lay away my helpmeet and my spouse
in a lone bed. So ended my repose.
Years we'd spent together in the same house

became beads to tell, the string broken—loose
time come unstrung. Still, outside, the spruce grows,
and it is nature to try to mend loss.
Under that old mansard that bent and rose

over the life we'd built, my blood still flows
in fever now and then. I make my truce
with flesh through these paid women whom I use.
Above us, guarding and graceful, the spruce

used to seem a symbol of common use
and fulfillment of self and heart—those blues
tipping sheer limbs sharply; strong and close
and clean, the bole and needles of pure hues. . . .
Suddenly, nothing was left.

—L. T.

For a similar form, see the GLOSE, as well as the SONNET
REDOUBLED and the CAROL.

RONDEL

French. Syllabic or accentual-syllabic. Thirteen lines of any
single length divided into three stanzas, two QUATRAINS and
one QUINTET. The poem turns on two rhymes and is built on

a two-line refrain. The first line reappears as line seven (7) and as line thirteen (13), which ends the poem. The second line reappears as line eight (8), which ends the second stanza:

lines	rhymes and refrains	lines	rhymes and refrains	lines	rhymes and refrains
1.	A—*refrain*	5.	a	9.	a
2.	B—*refrain*	6.	b	10.	b
3.	b	7.	A—*refrain*	11.	b
4.	a	8.	B—*refrain*	12.	a
				13.	A—*refrain*

Rondel of Charles D'Orleans
*To his Mistress, to succour his heart
that is beleaguered by jealousy.*

Strengthen, my Love, this castle of my heart,
   And with some store of pleasure give me aid,
For Jealousy, with all them of his part,
   Strong siege about the weary tower has laid.

   Nay, if to break his hands thou art afraid,
Too weak to make his cruel force depart,
   Strengthen at least this castle of my heart,
And with some store of pleasure give me aid.

Nay, let not Jealousy, for all his art
   Be master, and the tower in ruin laid,
   That still, ah Love! thy gracious rule obeyed.
Advance, and give me succour of thy part;
Strengthen, my Love, this castle of my heart.
            —ANDREW LANG

The RONDEL SUPREME is one line longer. The double refrain forms lines thirteen (13) and fourteen (14); thus, the last stanza would be a SESTET instead of a quintet, and the scheme would look like this:

9.	a
10.	b
11.	b

12.   a
13.   A—*refrain*
14.   B—*refrain*

Confessional

My ghostly father, let me confess,
First to God and then to you,
That at a window—do you know how?
I stole a kiss of great sweetness:

It was done without advisedness,
But it is done, not undone now.
My ghostly father, let me confess,
First to God and then to you.

But it shall be restored, doubtless,
For kisses one should rebestow,
And that to God I make this vow,
Otherwise I ask forgiveness,
My ghostly father, let me confess,
First to God and then to you.
                    —CHARLES D'ORLEANS

For examples of contemporary rondels, see Philip Dacey's
"Rondel" and X. J. Kennedy's poem of the same title in
Strong Measures (op. cit.).

RONDELET

French. Syllabic or accentual-syllabic. The first line is a re-
frain that reappears as lines three (3) and seven (7). The re-
frain is four syllables or two verse feet in length. The rest of
the lines (2, 4, 5, and 8) are eight syllables or four verse feet
in length. Line four (4) rhymes with the refrain. Lines two
(2), five (5), and six (6) have their own rhyme:

lines   *syllables, rhymes, and refrains*
1.   x x x A   —*refrain*
2.   x x x x x x x b
3.   x x x A   —*refrain*

lines	syllables, rhymes, and refrains
4.	x x x x x x x a
5.	x x x x x x x b
6.	x x x x x x x b
7.	x x x A —*refrain*

The Swift Replies

The swift replies
Fall from air to the ear in Spring.
    The swift replies
To the phoebe who sounds her sighs,
To dovecall, the catbird crying—
And when the owl goes questioning,
    The swift replies.

—WESLI COURT

RONDINE

French. Syllabic or accentual-syllabic. Lines can be of any single length. The rondine consists of twelve lines divided into two stanzas that rhyme *(Ra)bbaabR abbaR*. The *refrain* is the *first word or phrase of the first line;* it reappears as line seven (7) and again as line twelve (12), ending the poem:

lines	rhymes and refrains	lines	rhymes and refrains
1.	. . . R a—*refrain is the first word or phrase*	8.	a
2.	b	9.	b
3.	b	10.	b
4.	a	11.	a
5.	a	12.	. . . R —*refrain*
6.	b		
7.	. . . R —*refrain*		

RONSARDIAN ODE—*see* ODE.
ROUND—*see* ROUNDELAY.

ROUNDEL

An English form. Accentual-syllabic. Lines can be of any single length. Eleven lines are broken into three stanzas: a QUATRAIN, a TRIPLET, and a QUATRAIN, in that order. The poem turns on two rhymes and is built on one *refrain*. The refrain consists of the *first word or group of words* in the first line. The refrain (*R*) rhymes internally with the *last word of the second line*. Short scheme: *(R^{b}a)baR^b bab abaR^b*. The diagram:

lines	rhymes and refrain	lines	rhymes and refrain
1.	... R^b a—*1st line contains rhyming refrain*	8.	a
		9.	b
2.	b	10.	a
3.	a	11.	... R^b —*refrain*
4.	... R^b —*refrain*		
5.	b		
6.	a		
7.	b		

The Way of the Wind

The wind's way in the deep sky's hollow
None may measure, as none can say
How the heart in her shows the swallow
    The wind's way.

Hope nor fear can avail to stay
Waves that whiten on wrecks that wallow,
Times and seasons that wane and slay.

Life and love, till the strong night swallow
Thought and hope and the red last ray,
Swim the waters of years that follow
    The wind's way.
      —ALGERNON CHARLES SWINBURNE

For a contemporary example, see Loring Williams' "A Sad Old Sot" in *Poetry* (op. cit.).

ROUNDELAY

Though the definition of a roundelay is any simple lyric that utilizes a refrain, John Dryden invented a very complex set form: twenty-four lines, turning on two rhymes, in four sestet stanzas. Except for lines one (1) and two (2) of the first stanza and lines three (3) and four (4) of the fourth stanza, all lines are *repetons or refrains,* each reappearing at least once elsewhere in the poem, in a certain order:

lines	rhymes	lines	rhymes	lines	rhymes	lines	rhymes
1.	a	7.	A^1	13.	A^3	19.	A^4
2.	b	8.	B^1	14.	B^3	20.	B^4
3.	A^1	9.	A^3	15.	A^4	21.	a
4.	B^1	10.	B^3	16.	B^4	22.	b
5.	A^2	11.	A^2	17.	A^2	23.	A^2
6.	B^2	12.	B^2	18.	B^2	24.	B^2

Although Dryden's metric is trochaic tetrameter, assumedly the lines can be of any particular meter, in any single length:

Roundelay

Chloe found Amyntas lying,
   All in tears, upon the plain,
Sighing to himself, and crying,
   "Wretched I, to love in vain!
Kiss me, dear, before my dying;
   Kiss me once and ease my pain."

Sighing to himself, and crying,
   "Wretched I, to love in vain!
Ever scorning, and denying
   To reward your faithful swain:
Kiss me, dear, before my dying;
   Kiss me once, and ease my pain!

"Ever scorning, and denying
   To reward your faithful swain."
Chloe, laughing at his crying,
   Told him that he loved in vain.

"Kiss me, dear, before my dying;
    Kiss me once, and ease my pain!"

Chloe, laughing at his crying,
    Told him that he loved in vain;
But repenting, and complying,
    When he kissed, she kissed again—
Kissed him up before his dying;
    Kissed him up and eased his pain.
                    —JOHN DRYDEN

See also the ROUNDELAY in the LYRICS section.

RUBAI

Arabic. Accentual-syllabic. A *poem* consisting of one QUA-
TRAIN rhyming *aaba*. Lines are either tetrameter or pentame-
ter. A RUBAIYAT is a poem made of these quatrains used as
stanzas.

In the INTERLOCKING RUBAIYAT, the end-sound of line three
(3) in the first stanza becomes the rhyme in the second
stanza; the same is true for succeeding stanzas, each picking
up its rhyme from the third line of the preceding stanza. In
the *last* stanza, the third line takes its end-sound from the
rhyme of the first stanza. The schematic for a poem of four
stanzas would be:

lines	rhymes	lines	rhymes	lines	rhymes	lines	rhymes
1.	a	5.	b	9.	c	13.	d
2.	a	6.	b	10.	c	14.	d
3.	b	7.	c	11.	d	15.	a
4.	a	8.	b	12.	c	16.	d

Robert Frost's "Stopping by Woods on a Snowy Evening"
is the best known modern example of an interlocking rubai-
yat, though it has a variant ending. Other examples of con-
temporary rubaiyats are Gary Gildner's "Meeting My Best
Friend from the Eighth Grade" and Miller Williams' "Ru-
baiyat for Sue Ella Tucker" in *Strong Measures* (op. cit.). For

other forms that use interlocking rhyme, see TERZA RIMA and the TERZANELLE.

RUNE

A letter of the Anglo-Saxon alphabet. A CHARM poem that utilizes runes or runic lore. See "The Mystery" by Amergin.

SAPPHICS

A Greek form. Quantitative accentual-syllabics. Unrhymed. In English meters, a SAPPHIC LINE consists of eleven syllables and five verse feet, the central foot being a dactyl. The other four feet, two on either side of the central dactyl, are trochees. The rhythms of each line are *falling rhythms*—the accents of all verse feet fall on the *first* syllable—except where variations are allowed: a spondee can be substituted for a trochee in lines one (1) and two (2), feet two and five; and in line three (3), foot five—see the *italicized* portions of the diagram below.

A SAPPHIC STANZA is a QUATRAIN composed of three such lines plus one that is shorter, called an ADONIC: one dactyl followed by one trochee. There can be any number of stanzas in a Sapphic poem:

lines   *meters*

1.   xx *xx* xxx xx *xx*

2.   xx *xx* xxx xx *xx*

3.   xx xx xxx xx *xx*

4.   xxx xx

Sapphics

If mine eyes can speak to do hearty errand,
Or mine eyes' language she do hap to judge of,
So that eyes' message be of her receivéd,
    Hope, we do live yet.

But if eye fail then, when I most do need them,
Or if eyes' language be not to her known,
So that eyes' message do return rejected,
　　Hope, we do both die.

Yet, dying and dead, do we sing her honour;
So become our tombs monuments of her praise;
So becomes our loss the triumph of her gain;
　　Here be the glory.

If the spheres senseless do yet hold a music,
If the swan's sweet voice be not heard but at death,
If the mute timber when it hath the life lost
　　Yieldeth a lute's tune,

Are then human minds privileged so meanly
As that hateful Death can abridge them of power
With the vow of truth to record to all worlds
　　That we be her spoils?

Thus, not ending, ends the due praise of her praise:
Fleshly veil consumes, but a soul hath his life
Which is held in love: love it is that hath joined
　　Life to this our soul.

But if eyes can speak to do hearty errand,
Or mine eyes' language she do hap to judge of,
So that eyes' message be of her received,
　　Hope, we do live yet.

　　　　　　　　　　　　　—PHILIP SIDNEY

　　Sidney's meters are not easy to hear in these modern days;
perhaps they were never easy to hear. For a contemporary
Sapphic poem with the first and fourth lines scanned, see
"Visitor" in *Poetry* (op. cit.); see also Charles O. Hartman's
"A Little Song," William Meredith's "Effort at Speech," and
Timothy Steele's "Sapphics Against Anger" in *Strong Measures* (op. cit.).

SATIRICS

Satire is a minor subgenre of the literary genre of poetry; sat-
ire mocks things, lampoons or parodies them. The two

major forms of satire are the EPIGRAM and the LITERARY EPI-
TAPH. The epigram has been described as "terse verse with a
cutting edge":

On Maids and Cats

A nimble cat and lazy maid,
Breed household feuds and are no aid;
But lazy cats and nimble maids,
Beyond all doubt, are greater plagues.
Once, now and then, the cat may eat,
But snoops the maid in every plate,
And makes the purse and cellar low.
How e'er it hits, *there is no dough.*
                    —HENRICUS SELYNS

The pun, of course, is on the word *dough,* and pun is often
an element of satire. It may come as something of a surprise
to discover that "dough" is of so ancient a lineage as a syn-
onym for *money;* and, since dough baked is "bread," how
hep is hip?

The literary epitaph is similar, except that it is cast in the
form of an inscription for a headstone; it has been described
as "terse verse for the long gone."

This Morning Tom Child, the Painter, Died

Tom Child had often painted Death,
But never to the Life, before:
Doing it now, he's out of breath;
He paints it once, and paints no more.
                    —SAMUEL SEWALL

SKELTONICS, which are insistently rhymed dipodic lines,
have been discussed elsewhere as a vehicle for satire. Here are
a few lines by the inventor of the form:

Justice Now

Justice now is dead;
Truth with a drowsy head,
As heavy as the lead,

Is lain down to sleep,
And taketh no keep:
And Right is over the fallows
Gone to seek hallows,
With Reason together,
No man can tell whither.
No man will undertake
The first twain to wake;
And the twain last
Be withheld so fast
With money, as say men,
They cannot come again.
        —JOHN SKELTON

For an example of a long satire—on contemporary poetry—written in Skeltonics, see Wesli Court's "Odds Bodkin's Strange Thrusts and Ravels" in *Poetry* (op. cit.).

An opposite prosody is the NASHER, also used as a vehicle for mockery. HUDIBRASTICS are irregular tetrameter lines rhymed humorously in couplets. The FABLIAU, mentioned earlier, is a satiric form, as is the SIRVENTE, a lyric satire on religion or public matters.

Rough meters such as Skeltonics and Hudibrastics are modes of *doggerel* verse. The term doggerel has often been used in a pejorative sense to mean verse written by someone with little skill, but doggerel can be used deliberately for broad comic effect.

The following poem is made up of seven discrete but thematically related Gaelic epigrams by various ancient, anonymous authors. The form is heptasyllabic quatrains, rhyming or consonating *abab* or *abcb,* as in several of the Irish bardic rannaigheacht stanzas:

Gaelic Stanzas I

What, my Lord, shall I do with
Work enough to fill a cart?
How build from a thousand boards
A tight little house of art?

The wind is dark, howling hard,
Tossing Ocean's hoary hair.
Tonight the dragon-boats' horde
Will not char my white bones bare.

If the sere leaves were golden
In the forest in the fall,
And the sea's whitecaps silver,
Finn would have bestowed them all—

My patron gives no horses
For the poems I write now.
He grants beasts as best he can:
For an elegy, a cow.

The famished winter wind keens,
The lakes glitter, the brooks flash,
The hoarfrost chimbles the leaves,
The white combers froth and clash.

I can't tell with whom she'll sleep,
But I'm certain to the bone
That blonde, beauteous Etan
Will not go to bed alone.

Bell of chiming cold and clear
On a night of hurtling wind,
Much better to tryst with you
Than to tumble, hag-entwined!
                              —ANONYMOUS

See the section on SATIRICS in *Poetry* (op. cit.) for other epigrams and for P. J. O'Brien's satire, "Cartoon Show," on the Popeye television shows. There are many other satirical poems throughout this book. See also the SIRVENTE in the LYRICS section and CAPITOLO under TERZA RIMA.

SÉADNA *(sháy-na)*

Irish. Syllabic. A QUATRAIN stanza of alternating octosyllabic lines with disyllabic endings, and heptasyllabic lines with monosyllabic endings. Lines two (2) and four (4) rhyme; line three (3) rhymes with the stressed word preceding the final word of line four (4). There are two cross-rhymes in the second couplet. There is alliteration in each line, the final word of line four (4) alliterating with the preceding stressed word. The final syllable of line one (1) alliterates with the first stressed word of line two (2).

The poem (not the stanza) ends with the same first syllable, word, or line with which it begins. A simplified version:

lines	syllables and rhymes
1.	x x x x x x xa
2.	x x x x x x b
3.	x x x x *c x* xc
4.	x b x c x x b

SÉADNA MÓR (sháy-na moor) is the same except that lines two (2) and four (4) have trisyllabic endings.

SEDOKA

Parts of Wallace Stevens' "Thirteen Ways of Looking at a Blackbird," which is widely available and can be found in *Poetry* (op. cit.), look very much like MONDOS, KATAUTAS, or other Japanese forms, including the SEDOKA. The sedoka is a poem, not necessarily of the question-answer mondo pattern, that is made up of two katautas (5–7–7, 5–7–7 syllable count). A *turn* (as in the Italian SONNET and the TANKA) takes place between the two TRIPLET STANZAS. It can be a dialogue, but the poem is written by a single author:

Dialogue

I am wearing blue
in honor of the sky. Shall
you wear green to honor earth?

I will don rainbows;
I will wear snow on my back—
white, allcolor forever.

—L. T.

See the other Japanese forms for related structures, in particular the MONDO and the KATAUTA.

SENRYU—*see* HAIKU.

SEPTET

A stanza or poem consisting of seven lines in any meter, rhymed or unrhymed. The SICILIAN SEPTET is written in iambic pentameter measures, rhyming *abababa*. For other set forms and uses of the septet, see the sections on RIME ROYAL and the RONDELET. For examples of contemporary poems written in septets, see the various poems listed in *Strong Measures* (op. cit.). Here is a nonce septet:

> *Upon His Leaving His Mistress*
>
> 'Tis not that I am weary grown
> Of being yours, and yours alone;
> But with what face can I incline
> To damn you to be only mine?
>   You, whom some kinder power did fashion,
>   By merit and by inclination,
>   The joy at least of one whole nation.
>
> Let meaner spirits of your sex
> With humbler aims their thoughts perplex,
> And boast if by their arts they can
> Contrive to make *one* happy man;
>   Whilst, moved by an impartial sense,
>   Favors like nature you dispense
>   With universal influence.
>
> See, the kind seed-receiving earth
> To every grain affords a birth.
> On her no showers unwelcome fall;
> Her willing womb retains 'em all.
>   And shall my Celia be confined?
>   No! Live up to thy mighty mind,
>   And be the mistress of mankind.
>   —JOHN WILMOT

SERENADE—*see* LYRICS.
SERMON—*see* DIDACTICS, LITURGICS.
SESTAIN—*see* SESTET.

SESTET

A stanza or poem consisting of six lines in any meter, rhymed or unrhymed. The ITALIAN SESTET is written in iambic pentameter measures, and it rhymes *abcabc*. The SICILIAN SESTET is the same, but it rhymes *ababab*. The HEROIC SESTET, also written in iambic pentameter measures, rhymes *ababcc* or *abbacc*. For an example of a poem written in sestets, see Chidiock Tichborne's "Elegy: On the Evening of His Execution," quoted earlier in these pages. For contemporary examples, see *Strong Measures* (op. cit.). See also the STAVE.

The SEXTILLA, a Spanish form, is an *octosyllabic* sestet rhyming either *aabccb* or *ababcc*. The following poem is a *heptasyllabic* sextilla written in rocking meters—scanning it will not reveal whether its measures are headless iambs or tailless trochees. The scene it describes is a long building with a stanchion at each end in which rope is being manufactured. The spinners walk backwards, round and round, braiding the great ropes used by the sailing ships of bygone ages; rope is the central image of each stanza:

The Ropewalk

In that building, long and low,
With its windows all a-row,
  Like the port-holes of a hulk,
Human spiders spin and spin,
Backward down their threads so thin
  Dropping, each a hempen bulk.

At the end, an open door;
Squares of sunlight on the floor
  Light the long and dusky lane;
And the whirring of a wheel,
Dull and drowsy, makes me feel
  All its spokes are in my brain.

As the spinners to the end
Downward go and reascend,
    Gleam the long threads in the sun;
While within this brain of mine
Cobwebs brighter and more fine
    By the busy wheel are spun.

Two fair maidens in a swing,
Like white doves upon the wing,
    First before my vision pass;
Laughing, as their gentle hands,
Closely clasp the twisted strands,
    At their shadow on the grass.

Then a booth of mountebanks,
With its smell of tan and planks,
    And a girl poised high in air
On a cord, in spangled dress,
With a faded loveliness,
    And a weary look of care.

Then a homestead among farms,
And a woman with bare arms
    Drawing water from a well;
As the bucket mounts apace,
With it mounts her own fair face,
    As at some magician's spell.

Then an old man in a tower,
Ringing loud the noontide hour,
    While the rope coils round and round
Like a serpent at his feet,
And again, in swift retreat,
    Nearly lifts him from the ground.

Then within a prison-yard,
Faces fixed, and stern, and hard,
    Laughter and indecent mirth;
Ah! it is the gallows-tree!
Breath of Christian charity,
    Blow, and sweep it from the earth!

Then a school-boy, with his kite
Gleaming in a sky of light,
   And an eager, upward look;
Steeds pursued through lane and field;
Fowlers with their snares concealed;
   And an angler by a brook.

Ships rejoicing in the breeze,
Wrecks that float o'er unknown seas,
   Anchors dragged through faithless sand;
Sea-fog drifting overhead,
And, with lessening line and lead,
   Sailors feeling for the land.

All these scenes do I behold,
These, and many left untold,
   In that building long and low;
While the wheel goes round and round,
With a drowsy, dreamy sound,
   And the spinners backward go.
   —HENRY WADSWORTH LONGFELLOW

A sestet that utilizes the BOB (see BOB AND WHEEL) is the Scottish BURNS STANZA or STANDARD HABBIE (see RIME COUÉE).

For various uses and relatives of these forms see the SICILIAN OCTAVE, OTTAVA RIMA, ITALIAN SONNET, and SONETTO RISPETTO.

SESTINA

French. Syllabic or, in English meters, accentual-syllabic. Thirty-nine (39) lines divided into six SESTETS and one TRIPLET, called the *envoi*. The poem is ordinarily unrhymed. Instead of rhymes, the six *end-words* of the lines in stanza one are picked up and re-used, *in a particular order,* as end-words in the remaining stanzas. In the envoy, which ends the poem, the six end-words are also picked up: *one* end-word is buried in each line, and *one* end-word finishes each line. Lines can be of any *single* length; the length is determined by the poet.

The order in which the end-words are re-used is prescribed by a set pattern lying in the numerological sequence *615243*. If this set of numbers is applied to *each* stanza's set of end-words, it will be seen that these words appear in the succeeding stanza in this order. In other words, if the end-words of stanza one are designated *ABCDEF,* applying the set of numbers will give us stanza two, *FAEBDC.* Doing the same to stanza two results in the following:

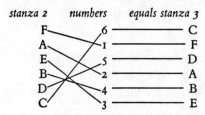

stanza 2	numbers	equals stanza 3
F	6	C
A	1	F
E	5	D
B	2	A
D	4	B
C	3	E

The numerological significance of the set, however, has evidently been lost since the Middle Ages, though the form is perhaps the most popular of the French Provençal forms in the twentieth century (though the VILLANELLE runs it a close second). Here is the schematic diagram:

lines	repeated end-words	lines	repeated end-words
1.	A	13.	C
2.	B	14.	F
3.	C	15.	D
4.	D	16.	A
5.	E	17.	B
6.	F	18.	E
7.	F	19.	E
8.	A	20.	C
9.	E	21.	B
10.	B	22.	F
11.	D	23.	A
12.	C	24.	D

	repeated		*repeated*
lines	*end-words*	*lines*	*end-words*
25.	D	31.	B
26.	E	32.	D
27.	A	33.	F
28.	C	34.	E
29.	F	35.	C
30.	B	36.	A

37.	B	E	
38.	D	C	} envoy
39.	F	A	

Not content with the considerable difficulty of writing the sestina as prescribed, Swinburne made the following verse rhyme and meter as well, thus turning its stanzas into Sicilian sestets:

Sestina

I saw my soul at rest upon a day
   As a bird sleeping in the nest of night,
Among soft leaves that give the starlight way
   To touch its wings but not its eyes with light;
So that it knew as one in visions may,
   And knew not as men waking, of delight.

This was the measure of my soul's delight;
   It had no power of joy to fly by day,
Nor part in the large lordship of the light;
   But in a secret moon-beholden way
Had all its will of dreams and pleasant night,
   And all the love and life that sleepers may.

But such life's triumph as men waking may
   It might not have to feed its faint delight
Between the stars by night and sun by day,
   Shut up with green leaves and a little light;
Because its way was as a lost star's way,
   A world's not wholly known of day or night.

All loves and dreams and sounds and gleams of night
   Made it all music that such minstrels may,

And all they had they gave it of delight;
  But in the full face of the fire of day
What place shall be for any starry light,
  What part of heaven in all the wide sun's way?

Yet the soul woke not, sleeping by the way,
  Watched as a nursling of the large eyed night,
And sought no strength nor knowledge of the day,
  Nor closer touch conclusive of delight,
Nor mightier joy nor truer than dreamers may,
  Nor more of song than they, nor more of light.

For who sleeps once and sees the secret light
  Whereby sleep shows the soul a fairer way
Between the rise and rest of day and night,
  Shall care no more to fare as all men may,
But be his place of pain or of delight,
  There shall he dwell, beholding night as day.

Song, have thy day and take thy fill of light
  Before the night be fallen across thy way;
Sing while he may, man hath no long delight.
                    —ALGERNON CHARLES SWINBURNE

New CollAge Magazine, Vol. 14, No. 1, 1982, edited by
A. McA. Miller, was a special "Sestina and Lines Issue," the
lines having mainly to do with discussing the sestina. In this
issue, Wesli Court published a sestina containing one or two
features that, as in the Swinburne example above, are not
traditional. First, the obsessive refrain, which is the first line,
contains all six of the end-words, but each time the line is
repeated the syntax is transposed by *hypallage.* Nonetheless,
the line always makes sense, and it reappears a seventh time
as a one-line envoy rather than as the normal three-liner, *but
with the sense of the original first line reversed:*

The Obsession

Last night I dreamed my father died again,
a decade and a year after he dreamed
of death himself, pitched forward into night.

His world of waking flickered out and died—
an image on a screen. He is the father
now of fitful dreams that last and last.

I dreamed again my father died at last.
He stood before me in his flesh again.
I greeted him. I said, "How are you, father?"
But he looked frailer than last time I'd dreamed
we were together, older than when he'd died—
I saw upon his face the look of night.

I dreamed my father died again last night.
He stood before a mirror. He looked his last
into the glass and kissed it. He saw he'd died.
I put my arms about him once again
to help support him as he fell. I dreamed
I held the final heartburst of my father.

I died again last night: I dreamed my father
kissed himself in glass, kissed me goodnight
in doing so. But what was it I dreamed
in fact? An injury that seems to last
without abatement, opening again
and yet again in dream? Who was it died

again last night? I dreamed my father died,
but it was not he—it was not my father,
only an image flickering again
upon the screen of dream out of the night.
How long can this cold image of him last?
Whose is it, his or mine? Who dreams he dreamed?

My father died. Again last night I dreamed
I felt his struggling heart still as he died
beneath my failing hands. And when at last
he weighed me down, then I laid down my father,
covered him with silence and with night.
I could not bear it should he come again—

I died again last night, my father dreamed.

—WESLI COURT

For an example of a double sestina cast as an ECLOGUE, see Philip Sidney's "Sestina" in *Poetry;* for a discussion by several teaching poets of a student's sestina, see Daniel Van Riper's "Fear and a Rose" in *Poets Teaching;* for contemporary sestinas and variants by various hands, see *Strong Measures.*

SEXAIN, SEXTILLA—*see* SESTET.

SHAKESPEARIAN SONNET—*see* ENGLISH SONNET, SONNET.

SHORT COUPLET—*see* COUPLET.

SHORT HYMNAL OCTAVE, SHORT HYMNAL STANZA, SHORT MEASURE, SHORT OCTAVE, SHORT PARTICULAR MEASURE—*see* COMMON MEASURE.

SICILIAN OCTAVE—*see* OCTAVE.

SICILIAN QUATRAIN—*see* QUATRAIN.

SICILIAN QUINTET—*see* QUINTET.

SICILIAN SEPTET—*see* SEPTET.

SICILIAN SESTET—*see* SESTET.

SICILIAN SONNET

A Sicilian OCTAVE (iambic pentameter lines rhyming *ababab*) plus a Sicilian SESTET with change of rhymes (*cdcdcd*) or an Italian SESTET (*cdecde*). See also the VOLTA.

SICILIAN TERCET—*see* TERCET.

SICILIAN TRIPLET—*see* TRIPLET.

SIRIMA—*see* CANZONE.

SIRVENTE—*see* LYRICS, SATIRICS.

SKELTONICS—*see* podics, SATIRICS.

SNEADHBHAIRDNE *(sna-vúy-erd-ne)*

Irish. Syllabic. A QUATRAIN stanza of alternating octosyllabic and tetrasyllabic lines ending in disyllable words. Lines two

(2) and four (4) rhyme; line three (3) consonates with them. Every stressed word in line four (4) must rhyme. Alliteration occurs as in RIONNAIRD TRI-NARD. The poem, not the stanza, ends with the same first syllable, word, or line with which it begins:

lines	syllables and rhymes
1.	x x x x x x (x a)
2.	x x (x b)
3.	x x x x x x (b c)
4.	b b (x b)

SOLILOQUY—*see* DRAMATICS.

SOMONKA

Japanese. Syllabic. The somonka is an epistolary love poem made up of two TANKAS (syllable counts: 5–7–5–7–7) and written by two authors. The first is a statement of love, the second a response. Though the following poem was not written by two authors, it is in the form of a somonka:

Epistles

I am writing you
from a pit. It is quite dark
here. I see little.
I am scratching this note on a stone.
Where are you? It has been long.

Thank you for your note.
I do not know where I am.
I believe I may
be with you. It is not dark
here. The light has blinded me.
—L. T.

SONG—*see* LYRIC.

SONNET

Accentual-syllabic. Roughly speaking, any fourteen-line poem written in rhymed, iambic pentameter verse. There are, however, two basic traditional patterns of the sonnet.

The Petrarchan or ITALIAN SONNET is divided into an OC-TAVE and a SESTET. The octave's rhyme is *abbaabba* (see ITAL-IAN OCTAVE); the sestet's rhyme varies, but it is generally either *cdecde* (ITALIAN SESTET) or *cdcdcd* (SICILIAN SESTET). A *turn* or *volta* traditionally occurs after the octave—a shift in thought that is pursued and closed in the sestet. "God's Grandeur" by Gerard Manley Hopkins, to be found in the early pages of this book, is an Italian sonnet in form though not in meter.

The Shakespearian or ENGLISH SONNET is divided into three SICILIAN QUATRAINS rhyming *abab cdcd efef* and one HEROIC COUPLET—*gg*. A *turn* takes place after the third quatrain and before the couplet, which is generally a climactic parallel.

There are innumerable other kinds of sonnets besides these two, however, and new varieties occur weekly, almost daily. The SPENSERIAN SONNET is a chain of three interlocking SICILIAN QUATRAINS, the second and third of which pick up their first-line rhymes from the last-line rhymes of the first and second quatrains, respectively, plus a HEROIC COUPLET: *abab bcbc cdcd ee*. The ENVELOPE SONNET rhymes *abbacddc efgefg* or *efefef*. For other sonnet forms, see the BLUES SONNET, BREF DOUBLE, SICILIAN SONNET, SONETTO RISPETTO, and TERZA RIMA SONNET. There are numerous examples of the sonnet in many collections and most anthologies, including those cited here.

The CURTAL SONNET, an invention of Hopkins, is an eleven-line form rhyming *abcabcdbcdc*. The first ten lines are iambic pentameter, but the last line is a single spondee. According to Dacey and Jauss, "the form is a truncated version of an Italian sonnet—its 'octave' being six lines long, and its 'sestet' being four and one-half." But it is not really a sonnet at all.

The HEROIC SONNET is an eighteen-line form that adds a heroic couplet to two stanzas of any kind of iambic pentameter OCTAVE or to four QUATRAINS.

The TAILED or CAUDATED SONNET adds two, three-foot tails and two heroic couplets to the Italian sonnet and rhymes *abbaabba cdecde e³fff⁵gg;* thus, it is twenty lines long.

The SONNET REDOUBLED is a chain of fifteen sonnets. *Each* of the fourteen lines in the *first* sonnet (the texte) becomes, in order, the *final* line in the following fourteen sonnets. A variation of this pattern makes each of the lines in the texte the *first line* in the following fourteen sonnets. For other forms that use a texte, see the CAROL, the GLOSE, and the RONDEAU REDOUBLED.

The CROWN OF SONNETS is a sequence of seven Italian sonnets. The *last line* of each of the first six sonnets becomes the first line in each of the ensuing sonnets; the last line of the seventh sonnet is the first line of the first sonnet. Since the seven sonnets are considered to be one poem, no rhyme word can be re-used except in the formally repeated lines, and new rhymes when they appear can not be those used elsewhere in the poem.

SPATIALS

The important thing in this subgenre or prosody (depending on one's point-of-view) is *how the poem looks on paper.* Thus, the typographical level is of great import when we consider SPATIALS or *spatial prosody.* There are two kinds of spatials: the CALLIGRAMME (shaped stanza, hieroglyphic verse) and the CONCRETE POEM.

The calligramme is, except for the shape of the stanza, an ordinary poem. It can utilize *negative* or *positive* shaping. According to Walter H. Kerr, author of "The View from Khufu's Tongue" in *Poetry* (op. cit.), "Positive shaping utilizes the words and negative shaping, the spaces. 'The View from Khufu's Tongue' is an example of negative shaping." This poem is a block of printed words with an empty space the shape of a pyramid in the center of the block. Here is an example of a calligramme:

The Pillar of Fame

Fame's a pillar here, at last, we set,
Out-during marble, brass, or jet,
Charmed and enchanted so
As to withstand the blow
Of violent overthrow
Nor shall the seas,
Or outrages
Of storms, overbear
What we uprear,
Tho kingdoms fall,
This pillar never shall
Decline or waste at all;
But stand for ever by his own
Firm and well-fixed foundation.

—ROBERT HERRICK

CONCRETE POETRY is ideogrammic spatials. For instance, in Japanese the characters for "rain" might be arranged on the page so that they *look* like rain falling. At the bottom of the picture, there might be the character for "house"; thus, the characters for rain are falling pictorially on the character for house. In an alphabetical language such as English, concrete verse is more difficult to write and not so immediately effective, as a rule, though Richard Kostelanetz managed to make the word "Nymphomania" completely effective in Chapter 5 of *Poetry* (op. cit.). The latter volume contains many other examples of both calligrammes and concrete poems, including Richard Frost's "Climbing the Tower at Pisa."

SPENSERIAN STANZA

English. Accentual-syllabic. A rhymed STANZA of nine lines consisting of eight iambic pentameter lines and one iambic hexameter line, called an ALEXANDRINE. The alexandrine is always the last (ninth) line of the stanza. There is no set pattern for the rhymes. Here is the first stanza of Alfred Tennyson's "The Lotos-Eaters":

> "Courage!" he said, and pointed toward the land,
> "This mounting wave will roll us shoreward soon."
> In the afternoon they came unto a land
> In which it seemed always afternoon.
> All round the coast the languid air did swoon,
> Breathing like one that hath a weary dream.
> Full-faced above the valley stood the moon;
> And like a downward smoke, the slender stream
> Along the cliff to fall and pause and fall did seem.

For another use of the alexandrine, see POULTER'S MEASURE. For a form of Spenserian stanza with a set rhyme scheme, see the HUITAIN.

SPLIT COUPLET—*see* COUPLET.

STANDARD HABBIE—*see* RIME COUÉE.

STAVE

English. Accentual-syllabic. Loosely, the STANZA of a hymn or of a drinking song, both of which often utilize refrains. Usually, lines are tetrameter or shorter. The term can be applied more specifically to a SESTET stanza made of three couplets and ending in a refrain: *aabbcC, ddeecC,* etc.

In a stricter version, both the first and last lines of each stave are the refrain. Thus, only the rhyme of the central couplet changes from stanza to stanza:

lines	rhymes and refrains	lines	rhymes and refrains
1.	A	7.	A
2.	a	8.	a
3.	b	9.	c
4.	b	10.	c
5.	a	11.	a
6.	A	12.	A

For an example of this kind of stave, see "Western Wind" in the section on the GLOSE. The strict stave is a variation of the COUPLET ENVELOPE: two couplets rhyming *a* enclosing another rhyming couplet: *aabbaa*.

Here is a simple stave that uses incremental repetition in a couplet refrain:

Corinna Singing

When to her lute Corinna sings,
Her voice revives the leaden strings
And doth in highest notes appear
As any challenged echo clear;
But when she doth of mourning speak,
Even with her sighs the strings do break.

And as her lute doth live or die,
Led by her passion, so must I,
For when of pleasure she doth sing,
My thoughts enjoy a sudden spring,
But if she doth of sorrow speak,
Even from my heart the strings do break.
                                    —THOMAS CAMPION

For other couplet forms, see COUPLET, DIDACTICS, FREE VERSE, CYWYDD LLOSGYRNOG, GWAWDODYN, HIR A THODDAID, RIME COUÉE, SESTET, and SHORT PARTICULAR MEASURE. See also, ENVELOPE STANZA.

STRAMBOTTO—*see* OCTAVE.

TANKA

A Japanese form. Syllabic. The tanka is a single QUINTET whose lines consist of five, seven, five, seven, and seven syllables, respectively. It is unrhymed:

lines	syllables
1.	x x x x x
2.	x x x x x x x
3.	x x x x x

lines	syllables
4.	x x x x x x x
5.	x x x x x

Note that the tanka is, in effect, a HAIKU (see TERCET) with two added lines of seven syllables each. For this reason, a separation is sometimes made between the third and fourth lines, making it a poem with one TRIPLET and one COUPLET. The first three lines are an independent unit that ends in a noun or a verb and after which a *turn* takes place: 5–7–5, 7–7.

The tanka has two forms (like the HAIKU and the SENRYU). In the second tanka form, called the WAKA, one subject is treated in the first two lines, another in the next two, and the last line is a refrain, paraphrase, or restatement: (5–7), (5–7, 7); the first *two* lines are a dependent clause or a phrase, the last *three* an independent clause, as the parentheses indicate. For an example of the tanka and the waka, as well as of other Japanese forms, see the poem titled "Paradigm" earlier in these pages.

A RENGA is a single tanka written by two authors. The first writes the triplet, the second writes the couplet response. A RENGA CHAIN is a poem made of a sequence of rengas and composed by a number of authors. The first triplet sets the subject, the succeeding couplet and all ensuing triplets and couplets amplify, gloss, or comment upon the first triplet. Renga chains can become extremely complex in many ways. For instance, a first triplet is written, and a couplet is added, completing the renga. Another triplet is added that follows logically, but that can also be logically read in place of the *first* triplet. A couplet is added, completing the second renga. A third triplet is added that can logically substitute for the second triplet. A couplet is added, completing that renga, and so on.

The term HAIKAI NO RENGA is applied to the humorous renga chain; it means, specifically, "renga of humor."

See also CHOKA, HAIKU, KATAUTA, MONDO, SEDOKA, and SOMONKA.

TELESTICH

An ACROSTIC made of final letters rather than initial letters.

TERCET

Can be written in any of the meters. Any complete poem of three lines, rhymed or unrhymed. The ENCLOSED TERCET rhymes *aba* (see ENCLOSED TRIPLET). The SICILIAN TERCET is an enclosed tercet written in iambic pentameter measures (see SICILIAN TRIPLET). See *Strong Measures* (op. cit.) for examples.

The TRIAD is a loose Irish form. It is a consideration of three things and their effect upon a person. See "The Rule of Three" earlier in these pages.

TERZANELLE—*see* VILLANELLE.

TERZA RIMA

Italian. Accentual-syllabic, usually iambic pentameter. Any number of interlocking, enclosed TRIPLET STANZAS. The first and third lines of a stanza rhyme; *the second line rhymes with the first and third lines of the following stanza.* In other words, the ending of the second line of any stanza becomes the rhyme for the following stanza: *aba bcb cdc,* etc. The poem usually ends in a COUPLET rhymed from the second line of the last triplet: *yzy zz.* The TERZA RIMA SONNET is a fourteen-line QUATORZAIN in iambic pentameter, rhyming *aba bcb cdc ded ee.* CAPITOLO is satirical terza rima.

For examples of terza rima, see Sylvia Plath's "Medallion," Robert Pack's "The Boat," Van K. Brock's "The Sea Birds," and Donald Revell's "Belfast" in *Strong Measures* (op. cit.). For a related form, see the TERZANELLE. Other interlocking forms are the INTERLOCKING RUBAIYAT and the SPENSERIAN SONNET. See also the MADRIGAL.

TETRASTICH—*see* QUATRAIN.

THRENODE, THRENODY—*see* CORONACH, DIRGE,
  LYRICS, MONODY.

THRIME—*see* TRIPLET.

TODDAID *(todd-eyed)*

Welsh. Syllabic. QUATRAIN STANZAS alternate between ten-syllable and nine-syllable lines. A syllable toward the end of the first line cross-rhymes into the middle of the second, and the same effect is reproduced in lines three (3) and four (4). Lines two (2) and four (4) rhyme with each other:

lines	syllables and rhymes
1.	x x x x x x *a* x x x
2.	x x x *a* x x x x b
3.	x x x x x x x x *c* x
4.	x x x *c* x x x x b

TRAGEDY—*see* DRAMATICS.

TRAGICOMEDY—*see* DRAMATICS.

TRIAD—*see* TERCET.

TRIOLET

A French form. Syllabic (in English prosody, accentual-syllabic). A poem consisting of a single OCTAVE turning on two rhymes. It is built on two refrains: line one (1) reappears as line four (4) and again as line seven (7); line two (2) reappears as line eight (8), completing the poem. The triolet rhymes *ABaAabAB*. Sometimes a separation is made between lines five (5) and six (6), making it a poem of two stanzas, a QUINTET and a TRIPLET. Lines can be of any single length:

lines	refrains and rhymes
1.	A—*refrain*
2.	B—*refrain*

lines	refrains and rhymes
3.	a
4.	A—*refrain*
5.	a
6.	b
7.	A—*refrain*
8.	B—*refrain*

Jasper Olson
(*from* Bordello)

I take my women any way they come—
I'm Jasper Olson, brother, hard and fast
I play this game. Though some folks think I'm dumb,
I take my women any way they come,
and come they do. There's no time to be numb
in this life—grab it now and ram the past.
I take my women any way they come.
I'm Jasper Olson, brother, hard and fast.

—L. T.

For other contemporary examples of the form, see *Strong Measures* (op. cit.): Barbara Howes' "Early Supper," Sandra McPherson's "Triolet," and Harold Witt's "First Photo of Flu Virus."

TRIPLET

A STANZA consisting of three lines. It can be written in any meter and can be rhymed or unrhymed. The ENCLOSED TRIPLET rhymes *aba*. The SICILIAN TRIPLET is an enclosed triplet in iambic pentameter measures. For examples, see *Strong Measures* (op. cit.).

There are two Welsh ENGLYNS that are triplet stanza forms; both are syllabic. ENGLYN MILWR (én-glin mée-loor) turns on one rhyme or consonance, and each line has a count of seven syllables. The rhymes change for each stanza:

The Head of Urien

I carry a severed head.
Cynfarch's son, its owner, would
Charge two warbands without heed.

I bear a great warrior's skull.
Many did good Urien rule;
On his bright breast, a dark gull.

I bear a head at my heart,
Urien's head, who ruled a court;
On his bright breast the crows dart.

I bear a head in my hand.
A shepherd in Yrechwydd-land,
Spear-breaker, kingly and grand.

I bear a head at my thigh,
Shield of the land, battle-scythe,
Column of war, falcon-cry.

I bear a head sinister.
His life great, his grave bitter,
The old warrior's savior.

I bear a head from the hills.
His hosts are lost in the vales.
Lavish it with cries and hails.

I bear a head on my shield.
I stood my ground in the field
Near at hand—he would not yield.

I bear a head on my greaves.
After battlecry he gives
Brennych's land its laden graves.

I bear a head in my hand,
Gripped hard. Well he ruled the land
In peace or in war's command.

I cut and carried this head
That kept me fearless of dread—
Sever my quick hand instead!

I bear a head from the wood,
Upon its mouth frothing blood
And, hereafter, on Rheged!

My breast quaked and my arm shook,
My heart was stone, and it broke.
I bear the head that I took.
—LLYWARCH HEN

ENGLYN PENFYR (én-glin pén vir) is a stanza whose lines consist, respectively, of ten (10), seven (7), and seven (7) syllables, rhyming AAA. One, two, or three syllables occur at the end of the *first* line *after* the *main* rhyme. These syllables are *echoed* by assonance, alliteration, or secondary rhyme in the *first few syllables of the second line*. The main rhyme *ends* the second and third lines:

lines	syllables and rhymes
1.	x x x x x x x x A b
2.	b x x x x x A
3.	x x x x x x A

The Corpse of Urien

The handsome corpse is laid down today,
Laid under this earth and stone—
Curse my fist! Owain's sire slain!

The handsome corpse is now broken
In the earth, under the oak—
Curse my fist! My kinsman struck!

The handsome corpse is bereft at last,
Fast in the stone he is left—
Curse my fist! My fate is cleft!

The handsome corpse is rewarded thus,
In the dust, under greensward—
Curse my fist! Cynfarch's son gored!

The handsome corpse is abandoned here
Under this sod, this gravestone—
Curse my fist! My liege-lord gone!

The handsome corpse is here locked away,
Made to rest beneath the rock—
Curse my fist! How the Weirds knock!

The handsome corpse is settled in earth
Beneath vervain and nettle—
Curse my fist! Hear fate rattle!

The handsome corpse is laid down today,
Laid under this earth and stone—
Curse my fist! This fate was mine!
                        —LLYWARCH HEN

For set forms and uses of the triplet or enclosed triplet, see also the sections on the TERCET, TERZA RIMA, TERZANELLE, TRIVERSEN, and VILLANELLE.

TRIUMPHAL ODE
A poem written in celebration of a victory. See OCCASIONALS, ODE.

TRIVERSEN
A native American form of variable accentuals is the TRIVERSEN STANZA, which was developed by William Carlos Williams and a number of others. Essentially, a triversen (triple verse sentence) stanza is partly grammatic in its prosody. One stanza equals one sentence. This sentence is broken into three parts, each part becoming a line composed of approximately one phrase. Thus, three lines (three phrases) equal one stanza (one sentence or clause). Williams, in attempting to explain this prosody, spoke of the "breath pause"—meaning only the process of breaking the sentence or clause into phrasal lines (see *line-phrasing*). He also spoke of the "variable foot"—the accentual element of the prosody: each line could vary in length, carrying from two to four stressed (but not necessarily alliterated) syllables. Here is the scheme of the first sentence of the following poem:

lines	words, accents, syllables, sentences
1.	x x x x x x xx
2.	x x x x
3.	xx x x x

Seed Moon
(from "Twelve Moons")

In the night there was a crescent
   thin as a breath
     floating in the sky.

Now the sun has quickened,
   it sprays the green meadows
     with drops of light.

Birds pierce the trees
   along the lake where grass
     thrusts through the bluff.

In the houses of the village
   there is the scent of savors—
     the women move and the men rise.

Soon the earth will fill with voices,
   the sounds of loam turning;
     the sun will stretch to fill the sky,

and in the woodland the deer
   will sample the air,
     lift their heads to listen.

—L. T.

The triversen proper (as distinguished from the stanza) is eighteen (18) lines long, as in "Seed Moon."

The theory behind the syllabic "emotive utterance" of the Japanese KATAUTA is analogous to this American prosody of the "breath pause." See also the HAIKU. Both theories postulate the three-line unit. See also the TERCET and the TRIPLET.

TROILUS STANZA—*see* RIME ROYAL.

TUMBLING VERSE—*see* SKELTONICS.

TWIME—*see* COUPLET.

VENUS AND ADONIS STANZA—*see* HEROIC SESTET.

VILLANELLE

A French form. Syllabic (in English meters, accentual-syllabic). Lines can be of any single length. Nineteen lines divided into six stanzas—five TRIPLETS and one QUATRAIN—turning on two rhymes and built on two refrains. The refrains consist of lines one (1) and three (3), complete. Line one (1) reappears as lines six (6), twelve (12), and eighteen (18); line three (3) reappears as lines nine (9), fifteen (15), and nineteen (19), finishing the poem:

lines	refrains and rhymes	lines	refrains and rhymes	lines	refrains and rhymes
1.	A¹—*refrain*	7.	a	13.	a
2.	b	8.	b	14.	b
3.	A²—*refrain*	9.	A²—*refrain*	15.	A²—*refrain*
4.	a	10.	a	16.	a
5.	b	11.	b	17.	b
6.	A¹—*refrain*	12.	A¹—*refrain*	18.	A¹
				19.	A²

There are several truly famous twentieth-century villanelles; "The House on the Hill" by Edwin Arlington Robinson, "Do Not Go Gentle into That Good Night" by Dylan Thomas, and "The Waking" by Theodore Roethke are perhaps the best known. The latter is included in *Strong Measures* (op. cit.), together with a dozen others by various contemporaries including Elizabeth Bishop, Marilyn Hacker, Richard Hugo, Donald Justice, Weldon Kees, and David Wagoner.

The TERZANELLE is of French and Italian derivation—an adaptation of TERZA RIMA to the villanelle form. It is nineteen lines long, composed of five interlocking TRIPLETS and a final QUATRAIN. Lines one (1) and three (3) reappear as refrains in the final quatrain. In addition, the middle line of each triplet is a repeton that reappears as the final line of the succeeding triplet, except the middle line of the last triplet, which reappears in the quatrain. The poem can end in one of two ways, as shown in the diagram:

lines	rhymes, repetons, and refrains	lines	rhymes, repetons, and refrains
1.	A¹—refrain	10.	d
2.	B —repeton	11.	E —repeton
3.	A²—refrain	12.	D —repeton
4.	b	13.	e
5.	C —repeton	14.	F —repeton
6.	B —repeton	15.	E —repeton
7.	c	16.	f
8.	D —repeton	17.	A¹—refrain or F —repeton
9.	C —repeton	18.	F —repeton or A¹—refrain
		19.	A² · · · · · A²—refrain

Terzanelle in Thunderweather

This is the moment when shadows gather
under the elms, the cornices and eaves.
This is the center of thunderweather.

The birds are quiet among these white leaves
where wind stutters, starts, then moves steadily
under the elms, the cornices, and eaves—

these are our voices speaking guardedly
about the sky, of the sheets of lightning
where wind stutters, starts, then moves steadily

into our lungs, across our lips, tightening
our throats. Our eyes are speaking in the dark
about the sky, of the sheets of lightning

that illuminate moments. In the stark
shades we inhabit, there are no words for
our throats. Our eyes are speaking in the dark

of things we cannot say, cannot ignore.
This is the moment when shadows gather,
shades we inhabit. There are no words, for
this is the center of thunderweather.

—L. T.

For another form that utilizes the repeton, see the PAN-
TOUM. Other interlocking forms are the RUBAIYAT and the
SPENSERIAN SONNET.

VIRELAI—*see* LAI.

WAKA—*see* TANKA.

WHEEL—*see* BOB AND WHEEL.

Appendix: Analytical Outline

Here is an outline of the topics covered in *The New Book of Forms:*

I. TYPOGRAPHICAL LEVEL.
A. *Mode.*
  1. Prose.
  2. Verse.
B. *Proportion in Figure.*
  1. Strophe.
  2. Stanza.

II. SONIC LEVEL.
A. *General prosody.*
  1. Accentual.
    a. Podic
  2. Syllabic.
  3. Accentual-syllabic.
  4. Isoverbal (wordcount).
  5. Grammatic parallelism.
  6. Syllabic-accentual.
  7. Invented prosodies.
    a. Moraics
B. *Specific prosody (i.e., "Normative accentual-syllabic").*
  1. Normative.
  2. Quantitative.
  3. Variable.
C. *Meter (if applicable; i.e., iambic pentameter, tetrapodic, octosyllabic, etc.).*
D. *Proportion in measure (differing line lengths, if applicable).*
E. *Proportion in rhyme (rhyme scheme, if applicable, including refrains).*
F. *Metrical variations (if applicable).*
G. *General form (ode, elegy, lyric) and specific form (sonnet, villanelle, nonce).*
H. *Other sonic devices (consonance, assonance, alliteration, etc.).*

III. SENSORY LEVEL.
A. *Tropes.*
  1. Descriptions.
  2. Similes.
  3. Metaphors.
  4. Rhetorical tropes.

B. *Usages and traditions of figures.*
  1. Metaphysical.   4. Surrealist.
  2. Symbolist.   5. Etc.
  3. Imagist.
C. *Emotional thrust.*
  1. Atmosphere.
  2. Mood.

IV. IDEATIONAL LEVEL.

A. *Subject (one word or phrase).*
B. *Schemas.*
  1. Orthographical.   4. Substitutive.
  2. Constructional.   5. Inclusive.
  3. Repetitional.   6. Exclusive.
C. *Viewpoint.*
  1. Egopoetic.
  2. Narrative.
  3. Dramatic.
D. *Syntax.*
  1. Subjective (egopoetic).   3. Dramatic.
  2. Objective (narrative).   4. Abstract.
E. *Level(s) of Diction.*
F. *Style (high, mean, base).*
G. *Theme (complete sentence).*

V. FUSION.

A. *Major genre.*
  1. Lyric.
  2. Narrative.
  3. Dramatic.
B. *Minor genre (if applicable).*
  1. Bucolic.   4. Satiric.
  2. Didactic.   5. Etc.
  3. Liturgic.
C. *Level(s) emphasized or balance of levels.*
D. *Proportion in treatment (means supportive of ends).*
E. *Value judgement.*

Index of Authors and Titles

Index of Terms

The forms of poetry are not included in this index because they are listed alphabetically in The Book of Forms and thus constitute their own index, complete with cross-references. They are also listed by the number of lines they contain in the Form-Finder Index. Thus, there are four indexes contained in this volume: (1) The Form-Finder; (2) The Book of Forms; (3) Index of Authors and Titles, and (4) Index of Terms. For cross references in small capitals, see the entry in The Book of Forms.